The Sleeping Beauty

A Pantomime

John Crocker

A Samuel French Acting Edition

SAMUELFRENCH-LONDON.CO.UK
SAMUELFRENCH.COM

Copyright © 1970 by John Crocker and Eric Guilder
All Rights Reserved

THE SLEEPING BEAUTY is fully protected under the copyright laws of the British Commonwealth, including Canada, the United States of America, and all other countries of the Copyright Union. All rights, including professional and amateur stage productions, recitation, lecturing, public reading, motion picture, radio broadcasting, television and the rights of translation into foreign languages are strictly reserved.

ISBN 978-0-573-16411-8

www.samuelfrench-london.co.uk

www.samuelfrench.com

FOR AMATEUR PRODUCTION ENQUIRIES

UNITED KINGDOM AND WORLD
EXCLUDING NORTH AMERICA
plays@SamuelFrench-London.co.uk
020 7255 4302/01

Each title is subject to availability from Samuel French,
depending upon country of performance.

CAUTION: Professional and amateur producers are hereby warned that *THE SLEEPING BEAUTY* is subject to a licensing fee. Publication of this play does not imply availability for performance. Both amateurs and professionals considering a production are strongly advised to apply to the appropriate agent before starting rehearsals, advertising, or booking a theatre. A licensing fee must be paid whether the title is presented for charity or gain and whether or not admission is charged.

The professional rights in this play are controlled by Samuel French Ltd, 52 Fitzroy Street, London, W1T 5JR.

No one shall make any changes in this title for the purpose of production. No part of this book may be reproduced, stored in a retrieval system, or transmitted in any form, by any means, now known or yet to be invented, including mechanical, electronic, photocopying, recording, videotaping, or otherwise, without the prior written permission of the publisher. No one shall upload this title, or part of this title, to any social media websites.

The right of John Crocker to be identified as author of this work has been asserted by him in accordance with Section 77 of the Copyright, Designs and Patents Act 1988

PRODUCTION NOTE

Pantomime, as we know it today, is a form of entertainment all on its own, derived from a number of different sources - the commedia dell'arte (and all that that derived from), the ballet, the opera, the music hall and the realms of folk-lore and fairy tale. And elements of all of these are still to be found in it. This strange mixture has created a splendid topsy-turvy world where men are women, women are men, where the present is embraced within the past, where people are hit but not hurt, where authority is constantly flouted, where everything is open to ridicule including pantomime itself at times and, above all, where magic abounds and dreams invariably come true. In other words, it is - or should be - fun. Fun to do and fun to watch and the sense of enjoyment which can be conveyed by a cast is very important to the enjoyment of the audience.

Pantomime can be very simply staged if resources are limited. Basically a tab surround at the back, tab legs at the sides and a set of traverse tabs for the frontcloth scenes, together with the simplest of small cut-out pieces to suggest the various locales, (or even just placards with this information written on them), will suffice. Conversely, there is no limit to the extent to which more lavish facilities can be employed.

The directions I have given in the text adopt a middle course and are based on a permanent setting of a cyclorama sky-cloth at the back, a few feet in front of which is a rostrum about two feet high running the width of the stage. About two thirds of the depth downstage is a false proscenium, immediately behind which are the lines for a set of traverse tabs. Below the false proscenium are arched entrances left and right with reveals if necessary to the proscenium. A border will be required at some point between the false proscenium and the cyclorama to mask lighting battens and the top of the cyclorama. Lastly there are sets of steps leading down into the auditorium at both the front corners of the stage.

Into this permanent setting are placed backing cloths or cut-out backings and various wings left and right (I have catered for one a side set on a level with the border, but a greater depth of stage may demand more for masking purposes). The frontcloth fly lines come in behind the traverse tabs. Cloths can, of course, be tumbled or rolled if flying space is limited. I have indicated that the traverse tabs should be closed before the end of most scenes to allow plenty of time for cloths to be lowered or flown; thus each scene can flow swiftly into the next, an important point if a smooth running production is to be achieved.

The setting and costumes should preferably be in clear bright colours to give a story book effect. I think it best to have everything in one period, apart from deliberate anachronisms in some sets and some of the comics' costumes.

As will be seen I have made various suggestions which point to the
mediaeval period since that seems to me the most suitable for this story. The
full armour worn by Sir Round and Sir Render in certain scenes should be light
in weight and Sir Render's must be fitted so that he can be helped out of it
very quickly after the explosion in Scene 3. If suitable armour cannot be
hired it can be simulated by stiff buckram painted silver, and if this is joined
by Velcro strips it can be very swiftly discarded. The Chorus costumes as
Hedge Spirits should be indicative of the various hedges named; Thorn of
Fire, by the way, is poetic (?) licence for Firethorn or Pyracantha.
Carabosse's disguise as a toadstool in Scene 10 requires only a dark cloak,
which as she sits on the floor with her back to the audience will look like
the stalk, and a large hat suitably shaped and stiffened and coloured bright
red with big white spots.

decided to make Daffy's costume specially. In either
case it should be fitted with torch bulbs in the nostrils, powered by a battery
and operated by a push switch in one hand. The other hand can operate the
powder bulb for the smoke effect. It should have a rubber tube leading to an
outlet between the nostrils. The water squirt in Scene 5 is worked similarly
by a water filled bulb.

Pantomime needs many props and often they will have to be home-made.
Instructions are given in the prop plot for any of the more awkward seeming
ones. Props should also be colourfully painted and in pantomime most of
them should be much larger than reality. It is also wise for the property
master to examine carefully the practical use to which a prop is to be put
for often a whole comedy sequence depends on something working properly.

I have not attempted to give a lighting plot as this entirely depends on the
equipment available, but generally speaking most pantomime lighting needs
to be full up, warm and bright. Pinks and ambers are probably best for this
and a circuit of blues in the cyclorama battens would be useful for the dawn
rise and dramatic effects generally. Follow spots are a great help, but not
essential. If they are available it is often effective in romantic numbers to
fade out the stage lighting and hold the principals in the follow spots,
quickly fading up the full lighting on the last few bars because this can help
to increase the applause! Flash boxes and the necessary flash powder,
maroons and the rain and cloud projectors can be obtained from the usual
stage electrical suppliers.

The music has been specially composed so that it is easy for the less
musically accomplished to master, but it is also scored in parts for the more
ambitious. If an orchestra is available well and good, but a single piano
will suffice. It is an advantage, however, if there can be a drummer as
well. Not only because a rhythm accompaniment enhances the numbers, but

also because for some reason never yet fully fathomed slapstick hits and falls are always twice as funny if they coincide with a well-timed bonk on a drum, wood-block or whatever is found to make the noise best suited to the action. A drummer can also cope with the "Tings" and "Whizzes" noted in the directions, though if necessary, of course, they can be done offstage. A special type of siren whistle can be got for the "Whizz" and the "Ting" requires a triangle.

Pantomime demands a particular style of playing and production. The acting must be larger than life, but still sincere, with a good deal of sparkle and attack. Much of it must be projected directly at the audience, since one of pantomime's great advantages is that it deliberately breaks down the "fourth wall". The actors can literally and metaphorically shake hands with their audience who become almost members of the cast; indeed, their active participation from time to time is essential. A word of warning on this, though - the actors must always remain in control; they must never encourage a response to such an extent that they can no longer be heard. This is particularly so in the case of hissing, which I think Carabosse should discourage. If her every appearance is drowned in a sea of hissing much of the effect of her part, and much of the plot too, will be lost. And the plot of a pantomime is of prime importance, precisely because the larger part of the audience, the children, know it and wish to see it faithfully followed. Therefore the producer should ensure that the story line is always clearly brought out and treated with respect and will find an emphasis on teamwork a help here, so that every member of the cast allows any other to be the focus of attention when theirs is the important bit in a scene. The selfish actor continually hogging the limelight is distracting to the audience and very aggravating to the rest of the cast! There is always room for local gags and topical quips in pantomime, but they should not be overdone. Nor, indeed, should any of the comedy - too much "milking" or too long dwelling on something which the cast think is hilarious but obviously the audience do not can slow down the pace disastrously, and much of this script should go at a pretty spanking pace. It should also be appreciated that any comedy scene needs rhythm and a shape; a big laugh in the wrong place can upset the balance and actually make the sequence as a whole less funny. Last, but certainly not least, the comedy must never appear to be conscious of its own funniness.

Characterization should be clear and definite. I prefer the traditional use of a man to play the Dame and a girl to play the Principal Boy. In the case of the Dame, anyway, there is a sound argument for this; audiences will laugh more readily at a man impersonating a woman involved in the mock cruelties of slapstick than at a real woman. For this reason an actor playing a Dame should never quite let us forget he is a man, while giving a sincere character performance of a woman; further, he can be as feminine as he likes but never effeminate. The Queen is a good-hearted soul with no pretensions to grandeur and is as merry as her spouse is sad. The King should not, however, seem to be sorry for himself and although frequently a ridiculous figure he should be capable of asserting authority when necessary, in Scene 7 for instance.

Like the Dame a Principal Boy also requires a character performance, but with the implications reversed, of course! An occasional slap of the thigh is not sufficient. Prince Ferdinand needs a light humorous touch, but he can also be very bold and romantic when the occasion demands. Lord Dan, the second boy, should also be thought of as a character part and should be played as a very gay and irrepressible light comedian.

Principal Girls can be a bore, but only if they are presented as mere pretty symbols of feminine sweetness. The Princess should have an infectious gaiety and an impish sense of fun. The more lively humanity she has the more touched an audience will be by her unfortunate fate at the hands of Carabosse.

Her adoring Pickles has, as he says, a serious mind. But his solemnity must at all times be endearing and never boring.

Spinning Jenny has a quick, shrewd mind. She is a typical Cockney and has all their appealing pertness.

Sir Round and Sir Render are "Gentlemen" as it were, knockabouts indeed but genuinely upper class nevertheless. Sir Round should preferably be a big, bluff, huntin'-shootin'-and-fishin' type, while Sir Render is weedier and more of a "silly-ass".

I have described Daffy in the text as spikily appealing and I do not think I can add usefully to that.

The Sleeping Beauty is very much a Fairy Story and therefore the Good and the Bad Fairies need very careful playing, with as much variety in their performances as they can muster. Both have a lot of comedy, but they must be able to become serious almost instantaneously. All Carabosse's actions are motivated by envy so her portrayal must be spiced with a good deal of genuine venom. Dreamawhile is tolerant and not easily ruffled, but though seemingly casual she is immensely competent.

I have made provision for a Chorus of ten, but naturally the number used will depend on how many are available.

JOHN CROCKER

CHARACTERS

LORD DAN OF DINI	The Court Chamberlain
KING COLE	
QUEEN COKE	
DAFFY	Her pet Dragon
SIR ROUND)	
SIR RENDER)	The Royal Champions
THE FAIRY DREAMAWHILE	
THE FAIRY CARABOSSE	A wicked Fairy
PICKLES	
SPINNING JENNY	
PRINCESS BEAUTY	
PRINCE FERDINAND	

CHORUS as Palace Servants, Royal Spinsters, Fairies, Courtiers, Suitors and Attendants, Hedge Spirits, Princesses and Spiders etc.

SYNOPSIS OF SCENES

PART I

Scene 1.	The Royal Palace in the Land of Merryspin
Scene 2.	Carabosse's Cavern and Dreamawhile's Dell
Scene 3.	The Royal Joust
Scene 4.	The Topmost Turret of the Tallest Tower
Scene 5.	A corridor in the Palace
Scene 6.	The Topmost Turret
Scene 7.	The Royal Palace

PART II

Scene 8.	Dreamland
Scene 9.	Pause for a Minim or Two
Scene 10.	Ye Olde Stirrup Cup
Scene 11.	In the Thick of the Thickest Thicket
Scene 12.	The Royal Palace
Scene 13.	Family Reunion
Scene 14.	The Royal Wedding Reception

Running time, excluding interval, approximately two hours, thirty-five minutes

THE SLEEPING BEAUTY

MUSIC 1.   OVERTURE

PART I

Scene 1   The Royal Palace in the Land of Merryspin

Fullset. A mediaeval Palace set in a castle. Backing on rostrum with step down in C. where there are double doors, with window L. and an aperture R. of them. The aperture is covered by a gauze panel painted to represent a tapestry. Wings L. and R. with castle decor. Line of three spinning wheels and stools R.C. Two thrones L.C. Dimly lit stage. MUSIC 2 plays softly.

A church clock starts to chime the hour, (orchestra), and a blonde CHORUS GIRL as a kitchen maid enters L. She yawns, stretches, rubs her nose vigorously then crosses and opens the doors. More light streams in, the church clock starts striking 7. She stands for a moment looking up at the sky, then picks up two bottles of milk, then two more and yet another couple all of which she hugs to herself with one arm. She picks up two more and realising her arm can accommodate no more puts

	them in the capacious pocket of her apron together with another two to keep them company, then holding a final one in her free hand she staggers L.
1st C.G.	You'd never think we had a baby in the house.
	(As she exits D.L., 2nd, 3rd and 4th CHORUS as servants enter R. rather sleepily with dusters and besom brooms, etc., with which they do a little desultory cleaning.)

MUSIC 2. (continued)   "THIS TIME OF DAY"

1st GROUP
> Seven o'clock in the morning
>> Is time we were waking
>> Give the old Palace a shaking
> At this time of day.

(5th, 6th and 7th CHORUS as servants enter L., also the KITCHEN MAID who collects more bottles. FADE UP LIGHTS as the others open curtains.)

2nd GROUP
> Seven o'clock in the morning
>> Is no time for slacking
>> On with our work and get cracking
> At this time of day.

BOTH GROUPS
> We have a Christening party,
>> A do to prepare for.
>> That's what those gadgets are there for –
> They're not meant for play!
> Let us prepare to commence now
>> To start to begin now
>> All the Royal Spinsters come in now
> At this time of day.

(LORD DAN OF DINI, the Court Chamberlain enters L. with remainder of the CHORUS as 3 Royal Spinsters who move in a dignified way to their spinning wheels, while the servants bustle in and out.)

SPINSTERS
> Spinning with thread that is golden
>> Is our occupation
>> That is the wealth of our nation
> In every way.

DAN
> We have a beautiful Princess,

Sc. 1 THE SLEEPING BEAUTY

                        A baby to christen.
                        No robe as lovely as this 'un
                        Has yet come your way.

SPINSTERS   Spinning is just the beginning.
                        To work and get weaving.

DAN   Time is a thief and it's thieving
                        The hours from the day.

                (Dance. The Groups unite.)

ALL   Seven o'clock in the morning;
                        A great day beginning.
                        We must get on with our spinning
                        At this time, at this time, at this time,
                        At this time, at this time, at this time of day.

DAN   Right, to work, to work. First you must –

2nd C.G.   Prepare the Royal Bassinette?

DAN   Yes.

2nd C.G.   Done.

DAN   Good. Then –

3rd C.G.   Polish the ceremonial crowns?

DAN   Yes.

3rd C.G.   Done.

DAN   Splendid. Then –

4th C.G.   Sweep the red carpets?

5th C.G.   Burnish the silver?

6th C.G.   Prepare the banquet?

DAN   Yes. Done?

4th, 5th & 6th C.G.   Not done.

DAN   Oh, pity.

                (2nd, 3rd, 4th, 5th and 6th C.G.s run off laughing.
                DAN manages to detain 7th with an arm round her
                waist.)

	I was hoping someone would have a moment for a little delightful dalliance.
7th C.G.	But you always hope that, Lord Dan. (She runs off laughing.)
DAN	True. But I can't change my nature just because we have a royal Christening today.
	(1st C.G. enters L. and crosses in front of him to doors.)
1st C.G.	Excuse me.
DAN	Certainly. I can't – (Turns to look after her.) Hm, new. (Turns back.) I can't alter my instincts just because we have to prepare to receive no less than seven fairy Godmothers. I can't –
1st C.G.	(returning with more bottles and crossing in front of him) 'Scuse me.
DAN	Of course. I can't – (Following after her.) Well, you can see I can't.
1st C.G.	Did you want something?
DAN	(eyeing her hair) Yes, I never could resist a little gold top. Gold! Good gracious! (Hurries R.) Lady Spinsters, is the last of the gold thread nearly spun?
1st SPIN.	Just one more lick –
2nd SPIN.	One more treadle –
3rd SPIN.	One more twist – and –
1st SPIN.	Yes, sir –
2nd SPIN.	Yes, sir –
3rd SPIN.	Three spindles full!
	(They hold them up.)
DAN	Splendid, then off with them to the weavers. They're waiting to finish her Highness's Christening robe.
SPINSTERS	(going off R.) At once, Lord Chamberlain.

1st C.G.		Why does she want a gold robe?
DAN		Well, it's a sort of symbol because all the country's wealth comes from spinning.
1st C.G.		Hm. I think gold would be cold.
DAN		Perhaps you feel diamonds would be warmer.
1st C.G.		Silly, diamonds would be too nobbly. That reminds me, there's a gent in a nobbly nightcap looking for you.
DAN		A gent in a nobbly nightcap?
1st C.G.		Yes, I had to chase him out of the kitchen. He tried to pinch my cream buns. (Exit L.)
DAN		Nobbly nightcap? Cream buns? Ah, she must mean the King.
KING COLE		(off L.) Lord Dan! Court Chamberlain!
DAN		Here, your Majesty! Prepare to receive our royal sovereign of Merryspin, His Merriness King Cole. (Makes a profound bow.)
		(MUSIC 3. The KING in a nightgown with a royal crest on it and a nightcap surmounted by a crown, hops on on his R. foot because his L. is slipperless. He is eating a cream bun.)
KING		Ooh, my left tootsie _is_ getting cold. You haven't seen a slipper have you?
DAN		No.
KING		Pity. Still, about the arrangements for today.
DAN		Ah yes, your Merriness.
KING		(sighing) I suppose you mean me. I would have to be the King of a country where the monarch is always supposed to be merry. Me, who was cursed as a babe to cry whenever I want to laugh. (Starting to sniffle.) When you come to think of it, it's rather funny. (Bursts into tears, takes a bite on his bun and stops abruptly.) Um, delicious. (Hopping away to L.) Now about the arrangements for today.

Sc. 1 — THE SLEEPING BEAUTY

DAN	(following) Yes, your Merri – your Majesty?	

(The KING stops.)

KING	(indignantly) I say – you're walking.
DAN	Er – yes?
KING	Well, I don't think that's fair. I'm hopping. I mean, I am the King and if I have to hop then everybody must hop. (Hops L.)
DAN	Certainly, your Majesty. (Hops after him on R. foot.)
KING	That's better. Now we're on an equal footing. Equal footing. (Sighs.) I've made a funny. (Sniffling.) Well, go on, laugh.

(DAN forces a laugh and the KING again dissolves in tears, until he takes another bite of bun and stops abruptly.)

I love a good joke, you know.

DAN	Er – yes. Now, as your Majesty was chewing, I mean saying –

(1st C.G. enters L. with a slipper and stares at them.)

About today's arrangements.

1st C.G.	Oi!

(They turn. KING hurriedly hides what is left of the bun behind his back.)

You left your slipper in my kitchen.

KING	Ah, thank you. (Puts out hand for it.)
DAN	No, no, you must return it to his Majesty properly – on a salver.
KING	(disappointed) Oh, must she?
DAN	Certainly, your Majesty. As your Chamberlain I must see that court etiquette is preserved. (To C.G.) Run and get – I mean, hop and get one, my dear.
1st C.G.	Hop? Me? (Sniffs.) I've grown out of

Sc. 1 THE SLEEPING BEAUTY

        hopscotch.   (She walks off L.)

        (KING returns bun to his mouth.)

DAN   You must excuse her, your Majesty. She's new, I haven't been able to – er – train her yet.

KING   Ooh, you naughty Chamberlain. I know your sort of training.   (Digs him in ribs.)

DAN   My – ?

KING   Yes, you're a rogue, aren't you?   (Digs again.)

DAN   Well –

KING   A lively young blade.   (Digs.)

        (1st C.G. enters with slipper on salver.)

1st C.G.   Here!

KING   (taking it)   Thank you.   (Digging DAN in ribs.) A spark, eh?   (Absentmindedly chews edible pom-pom on slipper.)   Hm, not as good as your last batch.   (Starts to put remains of bun on foot and realises.)   Oh.

1st C.G.   (shaking head and going off L.)   Nuts!

KING   (putting slipper on foot)   What does she mean? There aren't any nuts in this bun. Which reminds me, I'm very worried about the arrangements for my daughter's christening today. I mean, you may have noticed I'm rather partial to buns.

DAN   Partial! I mean – yes, partial. But I will ensure there is a large supply.

KING   No, no, it's the Fairy Godmothers I'm worried about.

DAN   That's all right, your Majesty, there shall be more than enough for all seven –

KING   Ah, now you've hit it. I want to make sure there aren't eight.

DAN   Only seven were invited, your Majesty, on your Majesty's particular instructions.

KING	I know. Only seven were invited to mine. But an eighth came. Carabosse. She was very put out at not being invited. My father said someone must have slipped up. And then she did.	
DAN	Did what, sire?	
KING	Slip up. On the skin of a banana I'd been eating. I thought it was very funny. I rocked my cradle with childish glee. I haven't had such a good laugh since. In fact, I haven't had a laugh at all since. She put that curse on me, vowed I wouldn't laugh again until I was a hundred and fifty and a day. (Sighs.) It put me right off fruit. But it gave me quite a taste for buns. So now you know what to do.	
DAN	Yes indeed, your Majesty. No bananas and plenty of buns.	
KING	No, no. I mean to safeguard my little daughter. Carabosse must at all costs be prevented from coming here today.	
DAN	Ah, leave it to me, sire. I'll put your Royal Champions on special security duty at once. (Hops L.)	
KING	(following him, walking) Good, good. But what are you hopping for?	
DAN	Because – (Realises.) Oh, er, yes. Silly of me.	
KING	Silly? Mad. (Digs him in ribs.) Hopping mad. (Dissolves in tears.)	
DAN	Ha-ha – very witty, sir, very – excuse me. (Exits L.)	
KING	Hm, nice fellow, but a bit humourless. Fancy not letting himself go on a good joke like that. I must remember it if I ever get to a hundred and fifty and a day, but that's not for another hundred and eighteen years, because it was my thirty-tooth birthday yesterday. Oh dear, I've made another funny. I do wish I didn't have such a keen sense of humour.	

Sc. 1 THE SLEEPING BEAUTY 9

        <u>MUSIC 4.</u>   "WHENEVER I LAUGH"

> Ho hum! Diddlee dum!
> Life is a bore when you look glum;
> But however I try,
> Whenever I laugh I cry.
>
> Whenever I see a comical thing
>   I recognise it as humorous;
> I'm always prepared to join in a joke –
>   Occasions round here are numerous!
> If anyone else should stand on a rake
>   Or sit on a pin by accident,
> I sit and I have a jolly good cry
>   While others all creak with merriment.
>
> Ho hum! Diddlee dum!
> Life is a bore when you look glum;
> But however I try,
> Whenever I laugh I cry.
>
> Though folk may choke at a dubious joke
> And chuckle and roar at Mothers-in-law,
> And giggle with glee at fellows like me,
>   Whenever I laugh – I cry!

(Exit KING R.)

SIR RENDER	(off L.) Sir Round!
SIR ROUND	(off R.) Sir Render!
	(MUSIC 5. SIR ROUND marches on from R. to C. <u>SIR RENDER</u> enters backwards from L. and bumps into the pommel of SIR ROUND's sword hilt.)
RENDER	(clutching himself) Ow! It's her! It's Carabosse! It's – (Sees SIR ROUND.) Oh, it's you. I say, I'm frightfully sorry. I mistook your pommel for –
ROUND	Yes, yes, never mind all that now. We must do things in their proper order. You young fellers nowadays seem to have no notion of chivalry. We always start with salutations. (Draws sword.)
RENDER	But we met just five minutes ago, when the Chamberlain was telling us about Carabosse.

ROUND	I don't care - salutations! Sir Render, fellow Royal Champion, Companion-in-Arms, I salute thee! (Salutes him smartly, touching his sword to his lips and then to the ground.)
RENDER	Oh - jolly good. And - er - hullo to you too. (Gives him a little wave.)
ROUND	No! You've got to salute me back.
RENDER	Have I? Oh, very well. (Moves behind SIR ROUND and salutes, soldier-like.)
ROUND	Now what are yer doin'?
RENDER	Saluting your back.
ROUND	Not my back, me back.
RENDER	Me back? Oh, you want me back?
ROUND	Yes, I want you back to salute me back.
RENDER	(turning round) Ah, back to back.
ROUND	No! Come back here. (RENDER shrugs and returns to his former position.) Now salute me back.
RENDER	I can't. You haven't got a back here. Your back's back there.
ROUND	(almost explodes, but controls himself) I am merely tryin' to get you to return my salute. So just say "I salute thee" and get on with it.
RENDER	(tugs sword out) I salute thee and get on with it. (Raises sword to lips and hits nose.) Ooh! (Bangs point down hitting ROUND on L. foot.)
ROUND	Wow! Me gout!
RENDER	(puts sword back in scabbard pinching finger) Ooh! I do that every time. Jolly painful. I don't think I'm cut out for chivalry.
ROUND	Nonsense. For the sake of our little Princess we must be ready in case this wicked old Carabosse turns up.

THE SLEEPING BEAUTY

	But we must fight fair and that means chivalry. Now, the first thing is the challenge. Have you got your gauntlet ready?
RENDER	Well, sort of. (Holds up a woollen mitten.)
ROUND	Sort of! A woolly mitten! (Takes it.) What the dooce is the good of that?
RENDER	Well, it keeps your hand jolly nice and warm.
ROUND	But how can you issue a challenge with it? What yer goin' to say? There, I challenge thee, I throw down my woolly mitten? I'd better check the rest of your stuff. Fetch your armoury.
RENDER	Righto. (Pulls on from L. a mediaeval pram.) It's in here.
ROUND	In there. In a pram!
RENDER	Yes, I'm very fond of it. I grew up in it.
ROUND	(shaking head) I don't know. Well, show me your armour.
RENDER	Righto. (Holds up a small piece of silvery knitting on large knitting needles.) There.
ROUND	That?
RENDER	Yes, I thought I'd run myself up a nice light little suit for the summer.
ROUND	But that tatty bit o' knittin' won't protect yer.
RENDER	It should do. I'm using steel wool.
ROUND	Well, have you got a decent helmet?
RENDER	Er - no, not until my geraniums are out. I'm using it as a hanging flower basket. I do love flowers. But I've got a temporary helmet. (Holds up a blue enamel saucepan.)
ROUND	What! That looks uncommonly like a saucepan to me. You can't go around in a saucepan. Apart from anything else, that blue's not your colour at all.
RENDER	I know, but it was the only six and seven eighths

saucepan I could find. Still, the rest of my stuff's all right. Well, my lance got a little bent. (Holds up a lance bent at right angles.) But it's jolly useful for fighting round corners. And my two handed sword. (Holds it up. A good two-thirds of the scabbard looks very floppy. He starts to put it down.) And my –

ROUND Wait a minute. Hold it up again.

(RENDER does.)

I thought so. It's flabby. Why have you got a flabby scabbard?

RENDER Ah, that was a little notion of my own. They're so heavy these two-handed swords so I lightened it. (Pulls the large-hilted sword out to reveal a very short blade.) Jolly good wheeze, what?

ROUND By gad, it's lucky for our little Princess that I'm here to protect her.

RENDER Ah, but you haven't seen my secret weapon. It was given me by a funny old magician chap called Potts. (Produces a pistol.)

ROUND What is it?

RENDER Well, I call it a pistol, by its initials, you see – (Pointing them out along barrel.) Potts Instant Shot Tosser Or Lobber. Potts says it's years ahead of its time. You just put this little metal ball and a sort of magic powder in here, (The breech.) then you pull this, (The trigger.) and the little metal ball shoots out at this end, (The handle.) or is it this end? (The muzzle.)

ROUND Stuff and nonsense! What harm could that do to anybody – a little metal ball the size of a pea?

RENDER Well, Potts said it could kill somebody. Not that I'd want to do that, of course.

ROUND I should think not! I mean, fightin's one thing, but killin' people! That's not nice, it's not chivalry. (Takes pistol.) Have nothing to do with it, my boy.

Sc. 1   THE SLEEPING BEAUTY   13

              I don't suppose it'll come to anything, anyway.
              (With the muzzle pointing straight up in the air he
              inadvertently pulls trigger. The bang considerably
              startles them.)   Tcha! Obviously gone wrong
              already.   (Throws it off R. A dead chicken
              descends from flies in front of them.)   Where did
              that come from?   (Throws chicken on the pram and
              pushes it off L.)   No, no, my boy, a thing like
              that could be the death of chivalry if it caught on.
              And chivalry's not what it was as it is - as it were.

              <u>MUSIC 6.</u>   "ONCE UPON A TIME"

ROUND   Once upon a time, in the bad old days
& RENDER   When benefits were fewer,
              We wrenched the wealth from the idle rich
                  To help the needy poower.

ROUND   The wicked Barons we would soak
                  With chivalrous intent,
              And give it to the humble folk
                  Less merely ten per cent.

RENDER   But now there would be a Union strike
                  And letters from the lawyers,
                If we should try to take from the rich
                  To help the poor employers.

BOTH   Once upon a time, if there should be
                  A damsel in distress,
              She called upon such chaps as we
                  To tidy up the mess.

RENDER   She opes her lattice wide, and thence
                  Her handkerchief she throws,
              Then we sort out the miscreant
                  And donk him on the nose.

ROUND   But now if a girl has gone astray
                  And we should try to stop her,
              She tells us to mind our own bloomin'
                            business
                  Or else she'll call a copper.

BOTH   Once upon a time . . . Once upon a time . . .
              Once upon a time.

	(They exit L. A motor horn is heard honking off R.)
QUEEN	(off R.) Mind out! Clear the way! I can't stop!
	(MUSIC 7. The QUEEN enters R. and whizzes across the stage on roller skates. She wears a feather boa and a high conical mediaeval hat and carries a shopping basket, which has an old-fashioned motor car bulb horn on the handle, on which she is honking.)
	Oh dear, I'm going to - (She disappears off L.)
	(EFFECT 1. A loud crash, and a cry from QUEEN. She trudges back with her conical hat severely crumpled.)
	I did. Well, that's the last time I do the shopping on roller skates. (She takes them off during following and puts them in the basket.) I thought they might save a bit of time, there's been so much to do with the Christening today. In fact -
	MUSIC 8. "CHORES"

>   I have worked without pause at my limitless
>   chores,
>   Such as sweeping and shaking the mat;
>   I have washed up the supper and made me a
>   cuppa
>   And opened a tin for the cat.
>   I have dusted the halls and washed out a few
>   smalls
>   And the bathroom is looking like new,
>   And the budgie's been fed and I've made up
>   the bed
>   And I've shaken some stuff down the loo.
>   I've been darning some socks
>   And run up a few frocks
>   Then I looked at the post
>   And I made me some toast
>   And I glanced at the news
>   And I cleaned a few shoes
>   And I polished the floor
>   Till my fingers were raw,
>   Since then I've been out shopping without
>   ever stopping,

THE SLEEPING BEAUTY

> My feet feel worn down to the bone;
> I've been up to my tricks since a quarter past six,
> And the rest of the morning's my own, my own
> The rest of the morning's my own.

But I'm always a bit behind, you know. Well, I nearly missed my own wedding even. I did, I was out getting my trousseau together and suddenly I thought, "Coo, I should be at the church getting married!" So I just grabbed the first things that came to hand and dashed off. Oh, I did have a funny trousseau. Two string vests and a pair of gents long woolly underpants. Still, I had a good laugh about it afterwards - and my husband had a good cry. Oh, I'm forgetting, you don't know who I am. You'll never guess. I'm the Queen.   (Turns shopping basket to show royal crest on side of it.)   Yes, my hubby's King Cole and I'm Queen Coke. How are you? No, don't worry, you needn't stand on ceremony with me, I don't mind you answering me back. How are you, all right?

(AUDIENCE reaction.)

That's more like it. Of course my hubby's ever so high class. Well, Kings always are, aren't they? But I only used to be the under pastry cook. Well, you see he's so fond of buns and things that he was always popping down to the kitchen for a little nibble. Yes, he said he found my touch irresistible - with pastry that is. Anyway, today's the Christening of our baby daughter. I mustn't neglect my other baby, though. That's Daffy, my pet dragon. I wonder where he is?   (Calls.)   Daffy! His real name's Daffyd 'cos he's a Welsh Dragon, of course, but our old Dragon Keeper had trouble with his teeth. Every time he called "Daffyd!" out they popped, both sets. Well, one day he gave himself a very nasty bite in the back-yard so now it's Daffy for short. He is a miniature dragon, anyway.   (Calls.) Daffy! And he's no trouble, except about one thing - leeks. Yes, at first he'd just have a leek anywhere,

THE SLEEPING BEAUTY — Part I

anytime. Well, being Welsh they're his favourite food. And I've brought him one today, so he doesn't feel left out of things. (Takes large leek from basket.) There! (Moves L. calling.) Daffy! Daffy! Come on, boy, lovely leek!

(MUSIC 9. DAFFY's long snout comes round a wing R., then gives an appreciative wiggle. His nostrils glow and emit two puffs of smoke. (Battery operated torch bulbs and manually operated powder bulb fitted in snout.) He trots on, a spikily appealing little fellow.)

Daffy, where are you?

(He gives a roar just behind her, which startles her. She turns holding leek behind her back.)

Ooh, you did give me a shock, dear.

(He rubs his head against her leg with affectionate enthusiasm. Rasping noise from orchestra.)

Yes, yes, good boy, but gently, love. (Rubs leg tenderly.) They can be a bit abrasive, dragons. Now you'll never guess what I've got for you, Daffy.

DAFFY	(nods eagerly and glows and puffs smoke)
QUEEN	Ah, ah, naughty boy.
DAFFY	(hangs head)
QUEEN	That's his little vice, he smokes a lot. (Pats him.) Never mind, dear, it's very useful sometimes. If I want a quick cuppa two puffs from Daffy and the kettle's boiling. Now here you are, dear, a lovely leek.
DAFFY	(grabs it eagerly and is about to devour it)
QUEEN	Oh no, dear, not here. In your Dragonry, remember.
DAFFY	(starts to run off R. with it)
QUEEN	Hold on a sec though, I've got you a packet of Polos for after. (Bends to burrow in basket.)
DAFFY	(returns and puts leek down just under her bottom. He eyes the leek longingly and starts to glow and to

Sc. 1 THE SLEEPING BEAUTY

smoke more and more)

QUEEN Well, otherwise those leeks do linger. Where are they? Oh, I say, it is warm in here.

DAFFY (raises his snout in ecstasy at the smell of the leek, which brings his glowing nostrils almost in touch with her rear)

QUEEN Wow!   (She leaps up clutching her behind and runs off L. where she quickly switches boas for one with a line attached to it and returns waving a large fan over her hind quarters.)   Oh, Daffy, I think you've severely damaged my prestige.

DAFFY (looks suitably abject)

QUEEN Now I'm all hot and bothered.   (She starts to remove her feather boa. Siren whizz and it whisks out of her hands and off L.)   Oi! Come back! I only bought you this morning. I wonder where it's gone?

DAFFY (shrugs and crosses to peer off L., shading his eyes with one paw)

(MUSIC 10.   Boa 2 crawls through at top of L. pros arch and moves downwards.)

QUEEN Quick, there it is!

(As they run to arch it disappears lower down.)

Now where's it disappeared to?

(MUSIC 11.   Boa 3 appears L.C. on top of floats moving R. DAFFY sees it and excitedly draws QUEEN's attention to it. It stops C.)

Ooh, yes. Ssh! We'll take it by surprise.

(They creep elaborately towards it.)

Now!

(As they pounce siren whizz and it whisks quickly R. and disappears, leaving DAFFY on top of the QUEEN on the floor. Boa 4 appears almost at once making its way up R. side of pros arch.)

It's over there! After it, Daffy!

THE SLEEPING BEAUTY   Part I

(DAFFY obliges by running over QUEEN. As he jumps up to try and reach it it quickly reverses, runs down and disappears. QUEEN staggers up to follow DAFFY and Boa 3 returns from R. to L. along floats. DAFFY starts towards it and collides with QUEEN. Boa 3 disappears and they pick themselves up.)

It'll be over there. Quick!

(They hurl themselves over to L. arch and wait expectantly. MUSIC 12. Boa 4 appears on R. arch making its way upwards.)

(To AUDIENCE.)   Where is it? Where is it?

(Guided by AUDIENCE they run R., but too late and return to C.)

Well, now where is it?

(MUSIC 13. Boa 5 descends from flies to dangle tantalisingly over their heads. The QUEEN gives DAFFY a leg up, but he misses it as it whisks out of sight again with a siren whizz and they collapse.)

Goodness gracious. It's more like a boa constrictor than a feather boa.

(MUSIC 14. Boa 6 streaks across the wing L. moving upstage. They give chase then see Boa 7 going out through window L. of the central doors.)

Oh, it's escaped.

(As they stand looking out of the window Boa 8 comes through the keyhole of the door and off R. They run after it and Boa 4 appears moving slowly up R. pros arch. They return D.R. and it zips out of sight through its top hole.)

Whew! I give up for the moment.

DAFFY   (pantingly agrees)

QUEEN   But I do want my fluffy feathers back.   (To AUDIENCE.)   Ooh, I wonder if you'd help me? When you hear its little tune and it comes out would you shout "Fluffy Feathers"? Would you, oh good.

Sc. 1 THE SLEEPING BEAUTY 19

> Just try shouting it now. After three – three.
>
> (AUDIENCE shout.)
>
> (to DAFFY)   Hm, not bad, but perhaps they'd do better if we rehearsed it properly.   (To R. pros arch.)   Fluffy, could you oblige us with a little rehearsal?
>
> (A little of Boa 4 pops out and then back again.)
>
> I think that means yes, so I'll just run off and you stay here, Daffy, and make sure they shout.
>
> (DAFFY nods as she runs off.)
>
> (off L.)   Ready!
>
> (MUSIC 15.   Boa 4 appears. DAFFY encourages AUDIENCE to shout. QUEEN runs on. Boa goes.)
>
> Well, I did hear it – just about. But this is a very big palace so you'll have to shout louder than that. We'll try just once more.   (She runs off.)   Ready!
>
> (MUSIC 16.   Boa 4 appears, DAFFY encourages the AUDIENCE to greater efforts. QUEEN runs on, Boa goes.)
>
> Oh yes, very good. Ta, Fluffy. And you, Daffy. I think you've really earned your leek now. Oh and – (Bends to basket, remembers and moves to other side of basket.)   – and here's the Polos.
>
> (Gives DAFFY an outsize packet of Polos, he jumps up and down excitedly.)
>
> Ah. It's the holes in the middle he likes. He blows smoke rings through them.

DAFFY   (nods happily, gives a couple of puffs and trots off R. with the Polos and the leek)

QUEEN   Now, you won't forget to shout whenever you see my fluffy feathers, will you? If they do forget you and the boys can remind them can't you, Charlie?   (Or whatever CONDUCTOR's name is.)

CONDUCTOR   Yes, of course.

QUEEN		Have you met Charlie, our royal bandmaster? Go on, dear, give them a thrill; show them what you look like.

(CONDUCTOR turns and bows to AUDIENCE.)

Not bad is he? Of course, I'm very fond of music, particularly a good massed choir. If there's something I'd really like to do it's conduct a massed choir. I suppose you haven't got one handy, Charlie?

CONDUCTOR   No, afraid not.

QUEEN   Never mind. I haven't really time now. There's a thing or three I ought to do before the Christening.

<u>MUSIC 17.</u>   "CHORES"   Reprise

So I mustn't stand chatting. The coconut matting
Has got to be shampoo'd and set;
I must just put the broom round the visitor's room
And must carry the cow to the vet.
Then I must have a bash with a packet of Flash
And some Spry and some Mum and some Min
And some Flip and some Flop and some Dip and some Dop
And some Goo and a bottle of gin.
There's the curtains to fix
And the pudding to mix
And the fire to be raked
And some buns to be baked
And potatoes to peel
For the afternoon meal
And the ice-cream to get
And the jelly to set,
There's the fridge to defrost and the cheese to get lost
And the baker and plumber to 'phone,
And unless there's a few little jobs I can do
Then the rest of the morning's my own.

(Dance.)

Sc. 1   THE SLEEPING BEAUTY

>   The rest of the morning's my own, my own,
>   The rest of the morning's my own.

(She exits D.L. KING hops on U.L. now fully attired except that slipper is missing from his L. foot. He is munching another bun.)

KING
I've mislaid the other one now. I wonder –

(LORD DAN hurries on D.R.)

DAN
Ah, your Majesty, the –

KING
You're walking again.

DAN
Oh.   (Hopping on L. foot.)   Sorry, sire. The Fairy Godmothers are here.

KING
How many? Not eight?

DAN
No, sire, only –

KING
Ah, splendid, then hop and find her Majesty and the Princess, and the Royal Nursemaids, and the Royal Champions – and my slipper.

DAN
Yes, your Majesty.   (Hops off L.)

KING
I wonder if I left it in –

(1st C.G. hurries on indignantly L. with slipper on salver.)

1st C.G.
Yes, you did!

(Throws slipper to him off salver and stalks off again. He catches it and puts it on.)

KING
That's a relief.   (Puts last piece of bun in mouth.) Pity she didn't bring another bun too.

(MUSIC 18.   LORD DAN hops on L. carrying a scroll, followed by SIR ROUND holding up a large sword and SIR RENDER with a large spiked bludgeon and 3 of the CHORUS as NURSEMAIDS carrying an ornate cradle. All are hopping.)

I say –

(DAN holds up his hand, music stops and all halt with one foot in the air.)

DAN	Sire?	
KING	(walking up to them) What are you all playing at?	
DAN	Well, as - oh.	
KING	No one likes a joke better than me, but this is supposed to be a dignified occasion.	
DAN	Exactly, your Majesty. Everybody <u>walk</u> properly, please.	

(Signals for music to start again. MUSIC 19. They process round ending with CHAMPIONS taking up positions on either side of doors and the CHORUS putting the cradle D.C. and then backing aside.)

Her Majesty the Queen and her Royal Highness, the Princess!

(MUSIC 20. CHAMPIONS and CHORUS bow and curtsey as QUEEN enters L. carrying a baby swathed in a long gold robe, followed by DAFFY and the 1st C.G. who carries a baby's bottle. The QUEEN signals to DAFFY who gives a puff of smoke, then plunges his snout into the cradle to warm the bedclothes, while the 1st C.G. proffers the bottle, but the QUEEN shakes her head. DAFFY withdraws his snout and the QUEEN places the baby in the cradle. KING and QUEEN sit on the thrones L.C.

KING	Right, all ready, Chamberlain.

(LORD DAN bows and backs to R. and reads from scroll.)

DAN	Her Royal Highness's Fairy Godmothers, the Fairies Beautiful, Graceful, Tuneful, Gleeful, Peaceful and Thoughtful.

(MUSIC 21. Six of the CHORUS enter as Fairies from R. Each makes a graceful greeting to their Majesties and moves round to form a group R.)

KING	We greet you on this happy day. My love, have you a word to say?
QUEEN	Yes, how de do? I'm nicely ta.

Sc. 1 THE SLEEPING BEAUTY 23

KING	Er – quite. Now, here's our daughter –
FAIRIES	(cooing over cradle) Ah!
KING	To whom, by custom of our land,
	As Fairy Godmothers you stand;
	Seven in number as should be
	For Babes who are of Royal degree.
	So, having welcom'd you to court
	I –
QUEEN	Half a mo, dear, there's one short.
KING	Not all that – oh, you mean too few.
	(Tries to count.)
	I get so muddled after two.
QUEEN	Well, one's been lost or p'raps mislain.
KING	How very awkward. Chamberlain!
DAN	Not guilty, sire. I didn't touch
	A single –
FAIRIES	Ooh!
DAN	That is, not much.
KING	Tut, tut! But never mind that now
	This Fairy you must find somehow.
DAN	At once, in person, sire. Sir Round,
	Go quickly see this Fairy's found.
ROUND	Right, I won't leave you in the lurch.
	Sir Render, go and make the search.
RENDER	What, me? But I'm not even sure
	Quite who it is we're looking for,
	Her designation –
ROUND	Title –
KING	Style –
QUEEN	You mean her name?
DAN	(consulting scroll) It's –
	(HOUSE LIGHTS UP. DREAMAWHILE enters on R. side of Auditorium.)

DREAMAWHILE	Dreamawhile.
(Moves to mount stage by R. steps.)
(HOUSE out.)

I fear you'll think I'm quite inept,
But truth to tell I overslept.
(Yawns.)
I'll have to get a loud alarm
To combat slumber's too sweet charm.
Still here I am.   (Sees cradle.)   Ah, let me peep.
The lucky babe, she's fast asleep.
(Yawns.) |
| QUEEN | Oh, you poor thing, you look quite done.
Have some tea? |
| KING | Or perhaps a bun? |
| DREAMAWHILE | No, really I'm quite wideawake.
So let us now our presents make.
Come Beautiful you first.

(Each FAIRY moves to cradle to make her gift.) |
| BEAUTIFUL | Sweet child,
My gift is beauty, undefil'd.
(Touches baby with wand. Music ting.) |
| GRACEFUL | As Graceful then, thy pretty face
I will enhance with wondrous grace.
(Touches baby. Music ting.) |
| TUNEFUL | Tuneful am I, so I decree
Thy voice like nightingales shall be.
(Touches baby. Music ting.) |
| PEACEFUL | As Peaceful my task's clear enow,
An angel's temper I'll grant thou.
(Touches baby. Music ting.) |
| THOUGHTFUL | Thoughtful's my name, my gift likewise;
I bring thee wisdom as my prize.
(Touches baby. Music ting.) |
| GLEEFUL | A mind too serious though's a shame
And so, since Gleeful is my name, |

Sc. 1   THE SLEEPING BEAUTY   25

>   I'll make my blessing three in one -
>   Wit,* laughter* and a sense of fun.*
>   (*Touches baby three times. Music ting on each.)

KING   Now that I call a gift most rare,
                  I wish she had a bit to spare.

QUEEN   Hush, dear, don't interrupt or cough,
                  You might put Dreamawhile right off.

>   (They look at her. She is standing with her head on
>   one side and her eyes closed.)

                  D'ye think perhaps a little nudge?

DREAMAWHILE   (looks up, smiles and shakes head)
                  Only thinking, trying to judge
                  Just what there's left for me to - hark!

>   (EFFECT 2.   Sound of rushing wind growing in
>   volume.)

KING   It's getting windy!

>   (LIGHTS START TO DIM.)

QUEEN   And quite dark.

>   (A drum beat starts.)

DREAMAWHILE   That rush of wind and beat of drums
                  Make very clear who this way comes -
                  Such signs do Carabosse denote!

>   (Cries of dismay.)

KING   Fill up the drawbridge! Raise the moat!

QUEEN   Call out the doors and lock the guard!

ROUND   Quick, lad! Push home the door bolts hard!

>   (He and RENDER push across the heavy door bolts.)

                  Now let her try and get through that!

>   (FLASH. Doors fly open (bolt retainers only painted on)
>   knocking SIR RENDER down. CARABOSSE is revealed
>   as a ghastly travesty of a fairy in a bedraggled black
>   ballet dress, black tights, long straggly black hair
>   topped by a lop-sided black crown and carrying a

	black wand. More screams and cries as CHORUS FAIRIES run off R. KING runs and hides behind throne, SIR RENDER behind ROUND. QUEEN and DAFFY run over to DREAMAWHILE and NURSEMAIDS drop back L. round DAN.)
CARABOSSE	Well, it says "welcome" on the mat. Your welcome though don't seem too rich.
QUEEN	Ooh, go away, you wicked witch!
CARABOSSE	I'm not a witch you silly – Queen. How dare you my true rank demean? I am a Fairy – you ask her.
DREAMAWHILE	Oh, yes, indeed, I quite concur. Dear Carabosse, always so charming, So modest, friendly and disarming.
CARABOSSE	And sucks to you, dear. (To others.) Still, you see I am a Fairy, though maybe A naughty one. (Chuckles and steps forward.)
ROUND	Madam, forbear! As Royal Champion I say beware! Take one more step and you will feel My trusty sword of sharpen'd steel. (CARABOSSE cackles and gives a little flick of her wand as he raises sword. The blade "breaks". RENDER huddles on the floor.) Magic, by Jove! Well, I could cuss, That's just not fair or chival<u>rous</u>. Sir Render – Good Gad, off the floor, It's up to you now.
RENDER	(rising nervously) Me? Oh lor'! (In a very high voice.) I challenge – Hum! (Low voice.) I challenge thee –
CARABOSSE	Well, high or low, fiddle-de-dee! (She waves wand and RENDER's bludgeon turns into a bouquet of flowers.)

Sc. 1   THE SLEEPING BEAUTY

RENDER	Ow, help I - ! Oh, they're rather nice. (Sniffs them appreciatively and sneezes.)
QUEEN	Daffy, get her, good dragon, mice! (DAFFY unwillingly steps forward growling feebly and emits a little puff of smoke, but when CARABOSSE raises her wand again he retreats hastily under the cradle.)
CARABOSSE	Now, where's that happy laughing King? (KING crawls from behind throne.) Glad to see me?
KING	(gulps) Like anything.
CARABOSSE	Then why did I not get, at least, An invitation to this feast?
KING	Well, I can't think - Oh yes, I can. It's all his fault.
DAN	Mine?
KING	Yes, Lord Dan, You know you're rankly inefficient.
DAN	But, sire, you said -
KING	(winking frantically) Now that's sufficient. Please do forgive the harm he's done. (Crosses R. to QUEEN.) Why, of all Fairies, you're the one The Queen and I most hop'd would bless Our little babe. So won't you?
CARABOSSE	Yes! I'll really make her heartstrings whirl. Just hear my gift for you, my girl. (She moves to cradle and with a yelp DAFFY runs off R. <u>MUSIC 22.</u> She waves her wand over the cradle.) The priceless virtues promis'd you You shall enjoy, as is your due. (All breathe a sigh of relief.)

But only till you reach eighteen!

(All gasp.)

And then a spindle sharp and keen,
A spindle on a spinning wheel,
A spindle like a shaft of steel
Shall prick your finger and you'll die!

(General consternation. QUEEN staggers back.)

QUEEN   Oh no! Oh no! Oh me!
(Backs onto a spinning wheel.)   Oh my!

KING   Your finger, dear?

QUEEN   No, in my case
A more - well - fundamental place.
(She rubs behind tenderly.)

(CARABOSSE cackles with laughter.)

Oh, yes, you think it's lots of fun.
But my poor babe! What's to be done?

DREAMAWHILE   (yawns and stretches)
Oh, sorry, pardon me, I'm sure,
But Carabosse is such a bore.
Don't worry, though.

KING   You mean - ?

QUEEN   She'll live?

DREAMAWHILE   Well, I have still my gift to give.

CARABOSSE   What? I've mistim'd my masterstroke!
But wait! No Fairy can revoke
A spell cast by another Fairy.

DREAMAWHILE   My dear Watson, that's element<u>ary</u>.
But nonetheless I have a scheme
To circumvent it with a dream.   (Moves to cradle.)
A dream of love that shall come true.
(Touches baby with wand. Music ting.)

CARABOSSE   Is that the best that you can do?
He-he! Hah-ha! Then I have won!

KING   Now look here -

Sc. 1   THE SLEEPING BEAUTY

CARABOSSE   Oh, go eat a bun!
               Ta-ta for now, enjoy your fears!
               I'll see you all in eighteen years.
               (With a cackle of venomous laughter she exits through double doors.)

DREAMAWHILE   She does so love to be dramatic,
               If a little overemphatic.
               But why do you all look so glum?

QUEEN   It's just that - well, a dream sounds - rum.

KING   Of course, we're very grateful, but -

DREAMAWHILE   You think my scheme will just go phut!
               Ah well, you'll see so just be brave.
               Meanwhile it might some trouble save
               To frame a law stamp'd with your seal
               Banishing ev'ry spinning wheel.

RENDER   Banish ev'ry - ! Oh, that's too utter!

ROUND   'Twill bring the country to the gutter.

DAN   We'd have to have a credit squeeze.

QUEEN   But what about our baby, please?

KING   Yes, yes, of course you're right my dear,
               There is no other course, I fear.
               The sacrifice must just be made.

DREAMAWHILE   How wise. I wish I could have stay'd,
               But I've another date to keep
               And that is with my beauty sleep.
               In eighteen years I'll be back too
               So not to worry. Toodleoo!
               (She exits happily R.)

               (Gentlemen bow as she goes out. All move D.S.)

KING   My love, my Chamberlain, my Champions   (To AUDIENCE.)   and my people, this is a solemn moment in the history of Merryspin. Hearken -

               (Close traverse tabs. Fly in Sc. 2 Frontcloth. Set remainder of scene.)

MUSIC 23.   SCENE FINALE

>Hear ye all!
>In order that no harm to our precious Princess may befall
>I decree –

(One of CHORUS enters R. with a parchment and a quill pen. QUEEN takes pen to sign.)

QUEEN	Proposed, seconded, signed and counter-signed by me,

(She pokes pen right through parchment when making a full stop.)

KING	That whereinas –
QUEEN	And hithertofore and thereinafter and notwithstanding and nevertheless and all that jazz.
KING	Throughout this land All spinning wheels, sewing machines, threading machines and similar apparatus incorporating a mechanically propelled needle are henceforth banned!
ALL	Such an Imperial Edict Is really most trying.
ROUND	Still there's no point in crying At this time of day.
RENDER	Since there is always tomorrow Our belts we'll pull tighter. Maybe the outlook is brighter
ALL	Some sunnier day.
QUEEN	Though we can't begin To tell you how much we appreciate the way you are all taking this on the chin,
KING	My dear good folk, Although we assure you this grieves we every bit as much as it does ye.
KING & QUEEN	We have spoke!

Sc. 2   THE SLEEPING BEAUTY

ALL   They have spoke, they have spoke.
KING & QUEEN   We have spoke!

(CHORUS sob noisily. All exit as –

BLACKOUT

Open traverse tabs.)

Scene 2   Carabosse's Cavern & Dreamawhile's Dell

Frontcloth painted to represent the cavern L. and the dell R. LIGHTS COME UP L. to reveal the dim and dingy cavern, which contains a small cauldron suspended over a fire and various bottles and phials on shelves. Also a large cuckoo-like clock.

MUSIC 24.   CARABOSSE is discovered sitting on a stool playing Patience at a table.

CARABOSSE   Hullo. Snug, isn't it, my den?
Well, fancy that! I've won again.
A tribute to my great resource
Because I use mark'd cards, of course.
They're so much easier for cheating,

(EFFECT 3.   Clock chime and a vulture comes out of clock door and croaks.)

But now I'll stop for time's a-fleeting.
It's nearly eighteen years, you know,
Since we met five minutes ago,
And really I can hardly wait
To see the Princess meet her fate.
But banning ev'ry spinning wheel
Was rather underhand, I feel.
I'd sneak one in, but oh, such malice!
They've put a guard all round the Palace.
But where the tallest tow'r thrusts high
Its topmost turret to the sky
One tiny window they've forgot!

And if I shrink myself a lot
I can fly in. But there's no spell
To shrink a spinning wheel as well.
Anything else is eas'ly done;
I even found a special one
For shrinking violets. So I need
A helper for my dirty deed.
One who'll a spinning wheel provide
And also get the thing inside.
(Consulting large book labelled "SPELLS".)
I'll brew a spell to draw one hither
With toe of newt and string of zither.

(As she prepares to do so LIGHTS FADE stage L. and COME UP R. on DREAMAWHILE's bright and cheery dell. MUSIC 25. It also contains shelves with various bottles and phials and a large clock, like a cuckoo clock but numbered from 1 - 20 round the dial and with only one hand, at present between the 17 and the 18. EFFECT 4. The clock begins to ring and a dandelion head pops out like a cuckoo and starts to waggle. A couch moves on from R. with DREAM-AWHILE asleep on it. She wakes and puts out a hand to stop the clock and yawns.)

DREAMAWHILE   What, time to wake again so soon?
This dandelion alarm's a boon,
It marks not only hours but years,
And Fairy time you see, my dears,
Goes such a pace that it's quite heady.
See - half-past seventeen already.
Time then that I was getting on.   (Rises.)
So for a while, dear bed, begone!
(She waves wand at it and bed trundles off R. She picks up a phial.)
Now, what's in here you'll never guess.
The stuff that dreams are made on - yes!
To credit which you might find hard,
As, indeed, might a certain bard.
But Dreamdust, as 'tis designate,
Will help the Princess to create
Her dreams of love that shall come true.
To give it and complete my coup

Sc. 2 THE SLEEPING BEAUTY 33

                    I shall dupe Carabosse and use
                    Someone whom she'd least think I'd choose;
                    For which the answer's plain, of course,
                    A copper from the local force!
                    I'll brew a spell to bring to hand
                    The nearest one to Fairyland.
                    (Delving among bottles and phials.)
                    One toe of newt, one zither string —
                    Be ready for a sudden ping,
                    You see the spell's completely muck'd
                    If the string's not freshly pluck'd.

                    (Twang from orchestra as she plucks one from a
                    bottle. CROSS FADE LIGHTS back to stage L. where
                    there is an answering twang as CARABOSSE extracts a
                    second one from her bottle.)

CARABOSSE   That's better. Now I cannot fail;
                    My first string must have been quite stale.
                    But now the spell begins to work —
                    She comes!

                    (Music whizz. SPINNING JENNY enters L. abruptly,
                    with a large triangular suitcase on which is inscribed —
                    "SPINNING JENNY. TRAVELLING SALES
                    CONSULTANT FOR PORTABLE SPINNING WHEELS.
                    H.P. TERMS ARRANGED.")

JENNY   Cor! I felt such a jerk!
                    And where am I and why and how?
                    I was in London Town * just now
                    Selling spinning wheels. What a shame!
                    Jennifer Hargreaves is my name,
                    Known in the trade as Spinning Jenny.
                    Well, round 'ere I shan't sell any.

                    (She sees CARABOSSE putting on what she imagines to
                    be a pleasant smile and beckoning.)

                    And 'oo's that there? Cor, what a face!
                    Did you want somethink?

CARABOSSE   Yes, my dear,
                    If you would please step over here.

                  * (Or wherever is most locally appropriate in 3 syllables.)

JENNY		(aside)　　Don't fancy it, but what the 'eck? P'raps I'll sell one to this old wreck. (Moves to her.) How de do?　　(Aside.)　　Better give it some pep. (Opens case to display spinning wheel.)

(MUSIC 26.)

I'm your friendly local travelling rep,
And it's spinning wheels what are my line,
For spinning coarse and for spinning fine.
Now this is our latest model 'ere,
Fitted with a special three wheel gear.
Our treadle, see, has a cushion'd grip,
The full-load spindle a knife-sharp tip,
And with ev'ry wheel we give quite free
A quarter pound of delicious tea.
Buy it outright, or as you'll have spotted
For easy easy terms sign on the dotted.
(Proffers a form.)

CARABOSSE　　Well, it's not me that's wanting one.

JENNY　　Now you say, when my nut I've done!
(Starts huffily to fasten case.)

CARABOSSE　　Wait!　　(Aside.)　　My true aim might make her
　　　　　　　　　　　　　　　　　　　　　　　jib,
Much better then for me to fib.　　(To JENNY.)
Now help you I both will and can.

JENNY　　Ho?

CARABOSSE　　　　Have you found a sort of ban
On spinning wheels in Merry-spin?

JENNY　　A ban? They won't even let me in.
I dunno why.

CARABOSSE　　(aside)　　Good.　　(To JENNY.)　　Well,
　　　　　　　　　　　　　　　　　　　　　　　I've plann'd
To shew them in that backward land
The wonders of the spinning wheel.
So first I must convert, I feel,
Their own Royal Family so dear.
And since, by chance, 'tis very near

Sc. 2   THE SLEEPING BEAUTY   35

           The birthday of their sweet Princess.
           I've vow'd . . .

JENNY   To give her one?

CARABOSSE   Why, yes!
           And that's where you could lend a hand.

JENNY   But they won't let me in the land.

CARABOSSE   Don't worry. I some necromancy
           Have learn'd for just that purpose.

JENNY   Fancy!

CARABOSSE   For getting in the Palace, though,
           Some slight disguise might help - I know,
           A Maid of Honour you'd best be.

JENNY   A Maid of Honour? No, not me.
           'Ere, wait a bit, that don't sound right.
           I mean, I don't speak proper.

CARABOSSE   Quite.
           (Picks up spell book.)
           But in this I'll find a solution.   (Turns pages.)
           Here we are - Instant Elocution!

           (As she starts brewing in her cauldron CROSS FADE
           LIGHTS to stage R.)

DREAMAWHILE   Lo, drawn hence by my potent spell,
           Here's a policeman at my -

           (A rather bemused looking PICKLES enters R., dressed
           in an overlarge and very colourful jester's costume.)

                              Well!
           I wish I knew some naughty oaths -
           No wait, maybe he's in plain clothes.

PICKLES   (looking around very puzzled)
           That's most peculiar, very queer.
           This can't be me 'cos I'm not here.
           Or am I? I still feel the same,
           Pickles still strikes me as my name.
           (Bends legs policeman-like. Sees FAIRY.)
           Excuse me, could you help at all?

	I've just lost a fancy dress ball.
DREAMAWHILE	Aha! A ball in fancy dress! A police ball maybe?
PICKLES	(bending legs again) How d'you guess?
DREAMAWHILE	Because then now I understand And welcome you to Fairyland.
PICKLES	You do? Excuse me while I think. (Steps away. Aside.) I've thought already. She's a kink. I'll humour her. (To her.) Then you're a Fairy?
DREAMAWHILE	That's right.
PICKLES	Well, I'm a dromedary, But in a masterly disguise.
DREAMAWHILE	(sighs) I do so wish I could tell lies – They're more convincing than the truth. Ah well, I'll have to be uncouth. (She taps PICKLES on his head sharply with her wand. Triangle ping.)
PICKLES	(indignant) Ow! Strike a policeman! How contrary! (Becoming suddenly placatory.) But quite all right since you're a Fairy.
DREAMAWHILE	Good. I've for you a special duty. To give this phial to Princess Beauty, And keep an unobtrusive eye To see no harm to her comes nigh. And for such purpose surreptitious, What costume could be more propitious?
PICKLES	What this? Oh no, it's much too large. Well, I borrow'd it from our sarge. And I'm not sure what Jesters do.
DREAMAWHILE	Some tumbling, tell a joke or two.
PICKLES	Oh no, I have a serious mind. I never make a joke, you'll find.

Sc. 2 THE SLEEPING BEAUTY 37

                      What else do they do? Ah yes, wait.
                      Of course - Jesters gesticulate.

DREAMAWHILE   You made a joke.

PICKLES   I did?

DREAMAWHILE   Just then.

PICKLES   They didn't laugh.

DREAMAWHILE   Well, try again,
   They will.

PICKLES   (shrugs)   Jesters gesticulate.

(DREAMAWHILE points wand at R. pros arch. A large
idiot board on which "HA! HA!" is written comes out.
DREAMAWHILE encourages AUDIENCE to obey it then
indicates with wand for board to go in, which it does.)

DREAMAWHILE   You see, of laughter quite a spate.
   Once more.

PICKLES   Jesters - er ... Move their arms?

(DREAMAWHILE points wand at pros arch again and
an idiot board on which "SILENCE" is written comes
out. She indicates for it to go in again.)

DREAMAWHILE   Spontaneity has its charms,
   But somehow something's wrong. Let's think.

(As they assume identical "thinking" positions LIGHTS
UP stage L. JENNY is just drinking a potion and
there is a row of empty glasses along table. The two
sides remain oblivious of each other.)

JENNY   Cor Blimey! That one tastes like ink!
   (Puts the glass down in line with the others.)

CARABOSSE   And the accent does not refine.
   Oh well.   (Starts to mix another brew.)

PICKLES   (hopefully)   Jesters make a sign?

DREAMAWHILE   No, no, it needs more -   (Breaks off to think
   what it needs.)

CARABOSSE   Pepper in,

	And just a tiny drop of gin. Now try it. (Gives a glass to JENNY.)
PICKLES	Ah! Jesters gesture.
JENNY	(in rather strangled genteel tones) Yais, that's a better one I'm sure.
CARABOSSE	Yes, yes, it is.
DREAMAWHILE	Much better, yes. But see if you can –
DREAMAWHILE & CARABOSSE	Force it less.
PICKLES	Jesters gesture?
JENNY	How now brown cow?
CARABOSSE	Oh yes,
DREAMAWHILE	You are,
DREAMAWHILE & CARABOSSE	Improving now.

(Close traverse tabs. Fly out cloth. Set following scene.)

MUSIC 27.   "SPELLBOUND"

DREAMAWHILE
They'll be spellbound, the Fairy story thickens.
They'll be spellbound, protest how they may.
They'll be spellbound, the tempo slowly quickens,
'Cos a plot involving Fairies has surprises all the way.

JENNY
She's a caution! I wouldn't try to stop 'er;
It's a knock-out to do as I am bid.
It's a giggle to find I'm talking proper,
And I ain't a 'doin' all the things I hadn't oughta did.

CARABOSSE
One thinks my drinks have awful savour;
But that idea is out of date,
'Cos nowadays it's strawberry flavour
Monosodium glutamate.

PICKLES	Make jokes like court jester, Be funny, dance and shout, Tell stories, make laughter – How I wish I knew just what on earth it's about

ALL	Spellbound, spellbound, spellbound,
	                                      spellbound!
	Spellbound, the Fairy story thickens,
	They'll be spellbound, protest how they may.
	They'll be spellbound, the tempo slowly
	                                      quickens,
	'Cos a plot involving Fairies has surprises all
	                                      the way.
	Spellbound, spellbound, spellbound,
	                            spellbound, spellbound!

(BLACKOUT. All exit. Open traverse tabs.)

Scene 3   The Royal Joust

The courtyard of a castle. Cut-out castellated backing on rostrum. Practical portcullis diagonally U.R., with handle and gear to work it – or ostensibly so – to L. of it. The spikes at the base of the portcullis should be cut out of foam rubber. This piece can be used, with suitable masking behind it, in place of a wing. Wing representing tower L. with a big bell in it, or hanging out from it, and rope to pull it. This wing also has an opening in it, covered by a gauze panel, which can be raised and lowered. L.C. a dais with two seats on it, and tapestry curtains backing it.

Some CHORUS discovered as female servants bustling about with mops and brooms and singing.

        MUSIC 28.   "HAPPY BIRTHDAY"

CHORUS	Happy birthday to our Princess,
	  We're assembled to give a cheer;
	For our Princess now is eighteen,
	  And she hasn't missed a year.

There'll be lots of fun and festivities
Time to love and to give it is.
    Everything is exciting and new,
It's a birthday – such a birthday,
    And we'll sing, "Happy Birthday to You".

(The KING and SIR ROUND and SIR RENDER enter L. with four more of the CHORUS bearing a canopy on four poles. As they sing the CHAMPIONS endeavour to get it erected over the dais but get it thoroughly mixed up with the KING in the middle of it. To do this consider the CHORUS holding the poles to be thus:-   A   B
   C   D

ROUND instructs A and B to change places which they do with A moving her pole under B's, while RENDER instructs C and D to change, which they also do with D moving under C. ROUND then tells A and C to change and C passes under A while RENDER gets B and D to change and B moves under D.)

ROUND   There'll be great display of chivalry,
    Wondrous feats of knightly rivalry.

RENDER   When the richest in the land
    Joust for our Princess's hand.

KING   There'll be lots of pomp and panoply
    When they've fixed this beastly canopy.

ALL 3   He who will the bravest ride
    Will claim our Princess for his bride.

ALL   Happy birthday to our Princess,
    And to enter here's her cue.
Happy birthday, happy birthday,
    We all sing "Happy Birthday to You".

(Pause.)

    Happy birthday to you.

(Pause.)

    Happy birth-day – to –

KING   Well, where is she? Dear, dear, just like her mother,

Sc. 3 THE SLEEPING BEAUTY 41

          always behindhand.

          (LORD DAN runs in from L. very agitated.)

DAN   Your Majesty, the Princess – She's gone! Disappeared!

          (General consternation.)

KING   What! Oh no! This is Carabosse's work!

ROUND   Leave it to us, sire! Render, sound the alarm bell!

          (RENDER pulls the bell rope, the big bell moves but only gives forth a tiny tinkle, <u>EFFECT 5.</u>)

KING   That's a fat lot of good.

ROUND   Don't worry, Your Majesty, we'll organise a search.

RENDER   Oh, jolly good. I'm a spiffing searcher. Well, I always win at hunt the thimble.

KING   Then search every cole and horner – er – every crook and nanny. Anyway, find her. Find the –

          (PRINCESS's voice heard singing off R.)

          The Princess!

DAN & CHAMPS   The Princess!

CHORUS   The Princess!

          (PRINCESS enters R. through portcullis with a small posy of flowers. CHORUS unwind the canopy during number and fit it over dais.)

          <u>MUSIC 29.</u>   "HAPPY BIRTHDAY"   Reprise

PRINCESS
        It's my birthday, happy birthday.
          I have not been eighteen before.
        For my birthday there's a party,
          And a party I adore.

OTHERS   There'll be lots of fun and festivities;
        Time to love and to give it is.

PRINCESS & OTHERS   Ev'rything's exciting to see and new.

        It's my/a birthday, such a birthday,

And And they/we'll sing "Happy Birthday to me"/you".

KING My dear child, thank goodness you're safe. But you mustn't go out alone and unprotected again. Not on your eighteenth birthday.

PRINCESS But I only picked some flowers, look. (Gives him flowers.)

KING Ah, there might have been spin – er – things out there – round triangular things.

PRINCESS Round and triangular? (Laughs.) How can they be both? Oh yes, I know something that is – in fact, I pricked my finger on it. (Sucks finger.)

(All gasp with dismay.)

A rose thorn.

(All sigh with relief.)

KING A rose thorn? I'm so glad – I mean – Anyway, we can't be too careful. Sir Round, double the guard immediately, call out the reserves.

ROUND At once, sire. Reserves, fall in!

(CHORUS fall in smartly, dressing by the R. etc.)

Shoulder mops and brooms!

(They do.)

To your posts – double march!

(They turn and run off R.)

Reserves posted, sire!

(DAN starts to sneak off R.)

KING Good. Pity we can't afford real soldiers nowadays, but – where are you going Chamberlain?

DAN I was thinking of joining the army, sire.

KING No, no, you must make sure everything's ready for all the suitors coming to joust for Her Highness's hand. I do hope the richest one wins.

Sc. 3 THE SLEEPING BEAUTY 43

ROUND I'm just goin' to give him a last practice run now, sire. Render, get your armour on.

KING What?

DAN (aside to him) Richest family in the land.

KING Really? (Fervently shaking RENDER's hand.) Jolly good luck, my boy. Have some flowers. (Gives them to him.)

RENDER Oh, thanks awfully, but I'm really much better at hunt the thimble. (Exits L.)

ROUND Nonsense. Magnificent horseman. Only got one little trouble. He keeps fallin' off. (Exits L.)

PRINCESS But I can't marry Sir Render. He's more like an uncle. Anyway, I don't want to marry just for money.

KING Of course not, my dear, but with the royal coffers so low, a handsome wedding settlement would be very useful. It might even help to pay for – oh no, that's a secret. Yes, Chamberlain –

(PRINCESS leans over to listen as KING whispers in DAN's ear.)

We're giving Her Highness a surprise present. It's a – (To PRINCESS.) Are you listening?

PRINCESS Oh no.

KING Good. (To DAN, whispering.) Where had I got to?

PRINCESS (whispering) About a surprise present for me.

KING (whispering) That's right. Thank y– You were listening.

PRINCESS Well, only a little bit. Just with one ear.

KING You mustn't. Cover up both your ears.

(PRINCESS does.)

(Whispering to DAN.) So I want you to sort out the candidates. (Bellowing to PRINCESS.) All right you can listen now.

THE SLEEPING BEAUTY   Part I

(PRINCESS uncovers her ears.)

DAN: Sort out what candidates, sire?

KING: (bellowing) For a Maid of Honour – I mean, (Whispering.) for a Maid of Honour for the Princess. (To PRINCESS.) You didn't hear that, did you?

PRINCESS: Not the second time you said it. But I think a Maid of Honour will be a lovely surprise. I shall go away and look forward to it now I don't know what it is. (She runs off L.)

KING: I've a feeling I muffed that somehow. Ah well, I suppose you can deal with the candidates?

DAN: Yes, Your Majesty, I rather think I can. (Exits L. rubbing hands eagerly.)

KING: Hm, maybe that wasn't such a good idea, either. Now, where's the Queen?

(MUSIC 30. Boa 4 appears from R. pros arch. AUDIENCE shout.)

QUEEN: (off R.) Thank you! On me way!

(Sound of bicycle bell and QUEEN enters through portcullis R. on a mediaeval bicycle and careers round stage.)

KING: (running after her) Stop! Stop!

QUEEN: I can't! They haven't invented brakes yet! (Falls off into KING's arms.) Ooh, it's still there. (Jumps up and makes a grab for Boa but there is a siren whizz and it whisks out of sight.) Drat! Missed it.

KING: My dear, I think we've got a nasty case of furry woodworm.

QUEEN: No, that's my new feather boa. Well, it was new when I lost it 18 years ago. They're all trying to help me catch it. (Picks up bicycle.)

KING: Well, I don't think you ought to go rushing about on that infernal machine. It's not good for the royal dignity.

Sc. 3 THE SLEEPING BEAUTY   45

QUEEN   You're so right, dear.   (Rubs behind.)   It's the
        wooden saddle, I think.   (Pushes bike off L.)
        I had to nip out and try and arrange for somebody to do
        the catering. I had a bit of trouble, though, - nobody
        would do it for nothing.

KING   What about our own staff?

QUEEN   Well, they're all busy womanning the battlements.
        There's only one thing for it - us.

KING   Us? But we must maintain our royal position. I mean,
        suppose anybody should see us?

QUEEN   Then we'll say it's a royal feast. Cheer up, I've got
        you a birthday present, and only a day late - that's not
        bad for me.

KING   A present? For me?   (Bursts into tears.)   That's
        made me very happy. What is it?

QUEEN   Guess.

KING   (warily)   It's not a massed choir concert, is it?

QUEEN   No, I'm giving you that next year. Try again.
        (EFFECT 6.   A deep-toned bell clangs off R.)
        Ah, somebody at the front drawbridge. It's probably
        your present. Come in!

KING   (rushing to let down portcullis)   No, no, wait!
        We can't have just anybody walking in. They might be
        spinning wheel smugglers.
        (PICKLES appears R.)

QUEEN   Look out!

PICKLES What for? Where?   (In looking round to see what
        it is he should avoid he trips over the traditional jester's
        pig's bladder he is carrying, and falls under the
        portcullis and is pinned to the ground by it.)
        Perhaps I've called at an inconvenient moment.

QUEEN   There, it is your present.

KING   What, that funny thing he's carrying?

QUEEN	No, all of him. He's a jester. I thought he might help to break that curse on you. After all, it's still got a hundred years to go.	
KING	Oh, I see. (Winds up portcullis again.)	
	(PICKLES starts to rise.)	
	In that case – wait a minute! (Releases portcullis which descends on PICKLES.)	
	(PICKLES falls on and bursts his pig's bladder.)	
PICKLES	I could call back, you know.	
KING	I must make sure he's bona fide. (Lies down to come face to face with PICKLES.) Are you bona fide?	
PICKLES	No, I'm Pickles. P.C. Pickles.	
KING	P.C.? Are those your initials?	
PICKLES	No, my rank.	
QUEEN	Rank? You're a jester, not a taxi.	
PICKLES	Jester? Oh yes, I am, aren't I?	
KING	Well, so you say, but what about spinning wheels?	
PICKLES	Spinning wheels? No, I don't do any juggling. I just – just jest.	
QUEEN	And a very good jester you are too, I'm sure. (Raises portcullis.) Up you get and do a spot of jesting now to prove it. The king loves a good joke, you know.	
PICKLES	(rising doubtfully) He does?	
	(QUEEN lowers portcullis with a bump behind him. KING rises.)	
	(Aside.) I could come unstuck here. Er –	
	(QUEEN gives him an encouraging smile, which he returns mirthlessly.)	
	Oh yes. (To them.) I say, I say, I – what's the next bit? Ah, I've got one. There was a young

THE SLEEPING BEAUTY

man - or was it a young girl? It could make a difference. I know! A riddle. Do you know the difference between a giraffe and a - a - well, something or other? No? Well, I shan't ask you to post a - that's it! The difference between a letter box and - and - whatever I said first, and the answer is I shan't ask you to post a zoo - er - come to the letter box. Well, anyway that's the funny bit. You get it?

(KING bursts into tears and exits L. howling.)

QUEEN   Oh, congratulations!

PICKLES   What?

QUEEN   Well done! (Pats PICKLES heartily on back.) That's the best cry he's had for ages. Ah, there's nothing like the sweet smell of success, is there? (Exits L.)

PICKLES   (shaking head puzzled) I wonder what went right there? That's the trouble with humour - it's not reliable; in fact, it's very funny stuff. I suppose there really are such things as jokes, but I've never seen one. I'll invent my own, I think; yes, a really good serious joke. But to work. I'm not here just for fun, you know. Oh no, I have to see the Princess is safe, keep an eye out for suspicious characters and give her the Dreamdust which I have safely in my pocket. (Puts hand as into a trouser pocket.) My pocket! (Patting himself all over.) I haven't got a pocket! Anywhere! Ah! (Feels under his tunic.) It's lurking in my jerkin.

(As he brings out the phial, which is enveloped by a very long label, the PRINCESS enters L.)

PRINCESS   Hullo.

(PICKLES turns to look at her and is stunned into stillness.)

I said hullo.

(PICKLES nods and waves.)

It's all right you can speak to me.

	(PICKLES opens his mouth several times like a fish but no sound comes out and he shakes his head.)
	Oh, please speak to me.
PICKLES	(gulps and turns away. Frantically to himself) Yes, speak to her, speak to her. But she makes me feel so – so. I must be – I am! And I can't even speak to her. Try something – anything. A simple little "hullo". (Tries it out in various ways.) Hullo. Hullo? Hu<u>ll</u>o. Hul<u>lo</u>. (Turns back to her and though he clearly mouths it no sound comes out. He shrugs and gives her a wave.)
PRINCESS	Perhaps you feel we should be introduced. I'm the Princess. Who are you?
PICKLES	(gulps and turns away again) The Princess? Then what's the use? They'll never make me a Prince. I don't know, though. Perhaps if I invented a really good joke they would. Prince Pickles the Priceless. Why not? I will then – I'll – I'll – Oh, I must give her this. (He struggles over to her and thrusts the phial into her hands and manages a strangled –) For you! (Dashes away from her to R.) I did it! I spoke! I said – (Crashes into wing R.) Ow!
PRINCESS	Oh, you poor thing.
	(PICKLES shrugs and smiles foolishly and staggers off R. then pops his head on again.)
PICKLES	Goodbye. (Disappears.)
PRINCESS	What a –
PICKLES	(popping head on again) I like you! (Goes.)
PRINCESS	Thank you. (Waving to him.) Goodbye. Well, that was –
PICKLES	(popping head on once more) Goodbye again! (He goes.)
PRINCESS	I wonder whose jester that is? One of the suitors, perhaps and he sent him to give me this.

Sc. 3 THE SLEEPING BEAUTY 49

(Unravelling the long label.) "For Princess Aurora Marina Miranda Christina Samantha Georgina Virginia Jane. Goodness, I'd almost forgotten those were my real names it's so long since anybody used them. Pity because they're nice names and they could have one for every day of the week and two on Sundays. (Unravelling more label.) Ah - "In brackets, Commonly known as Beauty." Exactly, I'm sure it's very common to be known as Beauty. It's certainly a great deal to live up to and just think - somebody might shorten it to Beaut. It doesn't say who sent it. (Throws long label off.) But what's on this tiny label? (Peers at it closely.) Dreamdust. (Unstoppers phial.)

(MUSIC 31. and LIGHTS BEGIN TO FADE as she sprinkles out a little of the gold powder and throws it up.)

Um - nice. Now what kind of man would have sent this? What would he look like? I know, like - like - (Throws up more powder.)

(MUSIC 32. FADE UP LIGHTS behind gauze panel in bell tower wing L., and PRINCE FERDINAND is revealed.)

PRINCE Like me.

PRINCESS Oh yes, yes!

(BLACKOUT to enable gauze panel to be moved for PRINCE to step out.)

Oh no, don't go, don't -

(LIGHTS UP.)

PRINCE I haven't, but keep thinking of me or I will.

PRINCESS Who are you then?

PRINCE (pointing to phial)   Just whoever you want me to be.

PRINCESS You mean I've invented you? My very own Prince? With this?

	(He gives a courtly bow.)
	But Prince who? Prince Claudio. (MUSIC 33 as she throws up a little more powder.) What's Prince Claudio like, Prince Claudio?
PRINCE	(drawing himself up and becoming rather haughty) Your royal Highness, it is my firm conviction that the formalities of the court should be maintained even between those of equal degree. Therefore, your royal Highness, I would suggest it preferable that your royal Highness should address me similarly as your royal Highness, does not your royal Highness agree, your royal Highness?
PRINCESS	No, she does not! Hastily scatters some more powder. MUSIC 34.) Let's try Prince, Prince – Prince Bill.
PRINCE	(mimes holding a pipe) Ah, my dear, have you seen my tobacco? I thought I'd just sit and read the evening paper till supper's ready. Something nice, is there? (Yawns and stretches.)
PRINCESS	No, that's a little too ordinary. I do think a Prince should be romantic. (Scatters some more powder. MUSIC 35.) What name would suit a romantic Prince?
PRINCE	Call me but love and I'll be new baptized.
PRINCESS	That rings a bell. Obviously Prince Romeo.
PRINCE	(kneeling fervently before her) It is my soul that calls upon my name.
PRINCESS	I have a feeling I should be on a balcony then you could say –
PRINCE	But soft! What light through yonder window breaks? It is the east, and Aurora Marina Miranda Christina Samantha Georgina Virginia Jane is the sun.
PRINCESS	(shaking head) No, your protestations won't scan if I'm not Princess Juliet. Pity. I rather liked him. But I could try another leaf from the same book. Yes, a gentle Prince – (Scatters some more powder.

Sc. 3 THE SLEEPING BEAUTY 51

<u>MUSIC 36.</u>) gentle Ferdinand.

PRINCE Oh yes, I like that best – or rather, I think I will – someday.

PRINCESS Someday?

PRINCE When I'm real, when I come true.

PRINCESS But will you ever come true?

PRINCE Of course, all the best dreams come true.

<u>MUSIC 37.</u> "YOU'LL SEE!"

You'll see! Soon a new day will dawn
When the best dreams will all come true.

PRINCESS You'll see! Some new star will be born
That will shine specially bright for you.

PRINCE Sweet dreams enfold you tonight when you rest,

PRINCESS Dreams of your lover for they are the best.

BOTH Tomorrow, when the sun will arise,
You will see your dreams before your very eyes
You'll see! You'll see! You'll see!

PRINCE Dream till the moment when your love is born,

PRINCESS Dream till the perfumed magic of the dawn.

BOTH Some day love will open your eyes
And then with ecstasy and wonder and surprise –
You'll see! You'll see! You'll see!

(LIGHTS START FADE.)

PRINCESS Don't go! Don't go!

PRINCE (backing away from her) I must. I must. All your Dreamdust is gone.

PRINCESS But I'll never see you again.

PRINCE (voice getting quieter and quieter) Oh yes, always. In your heart and in – in –

(END FADE in BLACKOUT. PRINCE exits.)

PRINCESS In my dreams.

(FADE UP LIGHTS.)

> Some day love will open your eyes
> And then with ecstasy and wonder and surprise -
> You'll see! You'll see! You'll see!

(PRINCESS runs off L. clasping her precious but empty phial of Dreamdust. MUSIC 38. JENNY creeps on R. to portcullis with her spinning wheel case, with its revelations of her name and trade now removed or covered over. She tries to raise portcullis.)

JENNY   Oh no, don't say I've got this far and now I can't get in.

(Flash and portcullis rumbles up.)

Oh ta. I wonder 'ow that 'appened?

(It thumps down behind her, which makes her jump. CARABOSSE gives a cackle of laughter off.)

Now I know. I suppose she is all right, that old girl. I'm beginning to think she's a bit - Now, Jennifer Hargreaves, don't get fanciful. This is the best chance you've ever 'ad so just get on with it. Right, she said to meet her in the topmost turret of the tallest tower, so I'll hide this here while I find the way to it.
(Puts spinning wheel case behind curtains of dais.)
And if I don't run into anybody I shan't 'ave to talk posh, so let's see if the coast's clear.

(MUSIC 39. As she creeps to look off D.L. enter DAN U.L.)

DAN   Hm, intriguing. I wonder if it's a game for one only or if I can join in.   (Moves behind her.)

JENNY   No one there.

(MUSIC 40. Both creep elaborately over to R.)

And no one there.

(DAN coughs loudly behind her. She shrieks and whirls round.)

Crikey! You didn't 'alf -   (In a very debbie

	drawl, but exaggeratedly stressing the false aspirates.) I mean, you did not 'alf give me ha shock, cock.
DAN	You've just given me one. Now I expect you are –
JENNY	Hi ham ha Maid of – sorry, hof Honour.
DAN	Well, roughly translated, I suppose that means you want to be one.
JENNY	No, Hi ham one halready.
DAN	But there haren't hany – sorry, it's rather catching. But you see, I'm the Court Chamberlain and I have to appoint the Princess's very first Maid of Honour today.
JENNY	(aside)　Well, that's a bit of luck.
DAN	You're the only candidate so far. What a pity, I should have given you the job right away if only –
JENNY	Hif honly what?
DAN	If only you spoke more naturally.
JENNY	Cor, thank 'eavens for that. I nearly strangulated meself.
DAN	Ah, that's more like it. In that case I think you're just what I – what the Princess is looking for. You've got the job. And to seal the appointment all new Maids of Honour are kissed by the Court Chamberlain. (Moves to do so.)
JENNY	(moving away)　Oh, why?
DAN	Well, because it's the custom of the court – a very old custom –
JENNY	Garn. I bet you just thought of it.
DAN	No, not just – about two minutes ago when I first saw you.
JENNY	Cheeky! – but nice.
	(She slips away as he again moves towards her.)
	Oh no, you'll have to give me a few better reasons than that.

THE SLEEPING BEAUTY   Part I

DAN   A few? I'll give you dozens.

<u>MUSIC 41.</u>   "REASONS FOR LOVE"

> There's your nose; there's the way you giggle,
> And you walk with a wicked wiggle -
>   That's to mention just a few
>   Of all the reasons for loving you.

JENNY
> You are full of the best excuses.
> I admit that I have my uses;
>   None the less I fail to see
>   You've any reason for loving me.

DAN   Your hair is soft.

JENNY   My toes turn in.

DAN   Your smile lights up.

JENNY   I've a double chin.

DAN   Your hands are small.

JENNY   My nose is bent.

DAN   Your shape is natural.

JENNY   - No comment!

DAN   Lips and eyes -

JENNY   I've two of each.

DAN   Your size is eight -

JENNY   That's a figure of speech!

DAN   With all the things you say and do   )
                     I've a dozen reasons for loving you.)
JENNY   I don't know if I quite agree   )(Together)
                     You've got any reason for loving me.)

(Dance.)

DAN   There's nothing could make you lovelier.

JENNY   You're absolutely right.

DAN   Your teeth are like the shining stars.

JENNY   You're wrong, they don't come out at night!

DAN	Love me please!	
JENNY	I am in a state!	
DAN	Just one kiss!	
JENNY	You will have to wait!	
DAN	With all the things you say and do	)
	I've a dozen reasons, dozen reasons,	)
	dozen reasons for loving you.	) (Together)
JENNY	I don't know if I quite agree	)
	You've got any reason, any reason,	)
	any reason for loving me.	)

(DAN chases JENNY off R. still endeavouring to get a kiss. KING peers on L.)

KING   Ah, all clear. Good, we can get on with the catering without anybody seeing us.   (As he goes.)
It's all right, my dear.

(MUSIC 42. Boa 4 appears on pros arch R. AUDIENCE shout. QUEEN runs on R. with a large pile of trick plates threaded together, but with one breakable plate loose on top.)

QUEEN   Oh, ta ever so.   (As she bends to put plates down Boa starts to go in and she straightens hastily.)
Stay there!   (It does. She puts a hand up gingerly towards it and the plates start to wobble so she wedges them with her chin and standing on tiptoe stretches up again.)   Nearly there, nearly - nearly -

(KING enters R. with a covered trolley on which are several teacups fastened down and one tiny cup with a hole at the bottom and a tank underneath. There is also a rubber tube pointing upwards fitted inside this cup. The other end of the tube is fitted onto the nozzle of a soda syphon which is attached to the back of the trolley. Also on the trolley is a large jug of milk and a plate of practical buns. The KING bumps into the QUEEN with the trolley. The Feather Boa goes as she teeters across the stage trying to steady the pile of plates. She drops the top loose one so that it breaks and in looking round to see what has happened

	nearly drops the whole pile over the edge of the stage. She manages to avoid this, but then trips and hurtles headlong off D.L. <u>EFFECT 7. Loud glass crash off L.</u> She re-enters without plates. KING moves trolley to R.C.)
	Oh well, we haven't got much to put on 'em, anyway.
KING	(with a hand hovering over the plate) There's these buns. And very delicious they look, too.
QUEEN	(tapping his hand) Now, now, naughty, naughty. That's all we've got to go round. (Moves behind trolley.) There's one thing we haven't thought of – how are we going to make the tea?
KING	Well, I think you have to boil some water and then –
QUEEN	I know that, dear – I mean, what in? We need something very big.
KING	Ah, I know something. Leave it to me. (Exits L.)
	(QUEEN picks up milk jug and whisks it over several cups till she is pulled up short by the tiny cup.)
QUEEN	Ooh, it must have shrunk. (Starts to pour milk into it.) I wonder what he's going to get?
	<u>(EFFECT 8. Loud clattering and banging off L.)</u>
	Doesn't sound as if it's just the kettle.
	<u>(EFFECT 9. Louder clattering and banging.)</u>
	Goodness, whatever is he doing? He's so impetuous, you know. (Realises she is still pouring into tiny cup to her surprise and continues staring amazed with little looks and shrugs to AUDIENCE, until the jug is empty.) Well I never, it's run out. (Looks in tiny cup.) That's funny, it's run out of here too. (Peers more closely.) Where's it gone to then? (She operates soda syphon with concealed hand so that a long jet shoots into her face.) Ow! I wish I hadn't asked now.
	(KING staggers on L. with a large steel looking cylinder, which has some broken off pipes sticking out

	of it.)
	What have you got there?
KING	The kitchen boiler. (Puts it down beside trolley.)
QUEEN	Ah, of course, ideal.
DAN	(off R.) Oh, please!
JENNY	(off R.) No!
KING	Someone coming. They mustn't see us doing this. Quickly, hide! (He gets behind boiler.)
	(QUEEN gets down behind trolley. After a beat the KING's hand comes out to take a bun, but the QUEEN's comes up and smacks it and both hands disappear. JENNY runs on R.)
JENNY	Cor, he ain't 'alf persistent. I'll get me case before he finds me again. Ooh, they look nice. (She takes a bun as she moves to R. of dais.)
	(KING's fist appears momentarily shaking angrily. DAN enters R.)
DAN	Coo-ee!
JENNY	Here we go again. (She runs round behind dais.)
	(DAN runs over, but realises buns when he has just passed them and runs back to get one. KING's shaking fist appears momentarily again. DAN runs behind dais. JENNY comes through curtains and as DAN reappears on L. of dais she goes back through them.)
DAN	That's odd. She's gone. (He retreats behind dais.)
	(JENNY reappears through curtains.)
JENNY	Fooled 'im! (Runs off L.)
	(Enter PICKLES R.)
PICKLES	What striking looking buns. (He puts out a hand for one.)
	(QUEEN's hand comes up and smacks his. KING's hand

	appears giving a thumbs up sign.)
	Ow! They are too.
DAN	(reappearing on R. of dais) I know, she's running round and round too. (Creeps behind dais again.)
PICKLES	Hullo, who's he and what's he up to?
	(DAN appears L. of dais, stops suddenly and jumps to look behind it, jumps to look in front of it then behind it again and creeps elaborately round the front to the back. As he does so—)
	Very suspicious behaviour. (Moves covertly over to behind dais.)
DAN	(appearing from behind dais) Well, she must have gone this way. (Exits L.)
PICKLES	(putting head out from behind dais and looking after him) I'd better keep an eye on him. (He creeps off L.)
	(KING and QUEEN emerge.)
KING	Beasts! Rotten-hide-and-seek-playing, bun-pinching beasts!
QUEEN	Never mind, dear. I'll bake a special batch tonight just for you. But we must get on and make the tea. How are we going to light the boiler?
KING	Er – with a match?
QUEEN	But there's nothing in it to light. I know – Daffy. We'll put him in the boiler. Let's fetch him.
	(They start to move L. and stop.)
KING	No! Here they come again.
	(They dodge back to their hiding places. KING comes out to take bun plate, QUEEN pops up and takes it from him. JENNY runs on from L. and goes to dais.)
JENNY	Now for my –
DAN	(looking on L.) Aha!
	(JENNY runs off R. DAN runs on L. and off R. after

	Sc. 3 THE SLEEPING BEAUTY

	her. PICKLES runs on after him.)
PICKLES	He's definitely up to no good. He's creeping very quickly now. (Runs off R.)
	(KING and QUEEN re-emerge. QUEEN puts bun plate back on trolley and they hurry L.)
QUEEN	Quick, we'll get Daffy before they –
ROUND	(off L.) Render!
KING	Back again!
	(They return hurriedly to their hiding places as SIR ROUND enters in full armour trying out a few passes with his sword.)
ROUND	Come on, Render, time for our practice bout. (Inadvertently spears a bun on sword.) Oh. How jolly nice. Render! (Exits L.)
	(KING and QUEEN are about to emerge when PICKLES returns from R.)
PICKLES	He's given me the slip. He must have doubled back.
	(As he crosses L., DAFFY enters after him. DAN appears through pass door R. of auditorium. (The following directions – given from the actors' point of view – assume an auditorium with aisles at each side and transverse aisles back and front, pass doors at L. and R. and exit doors L. and R. at the back. Naturally a different layout will require the business to be suitably adapted.) HOUSELIGHTS UP. At the same moment KING and QUEEN are crawling on all fours towards R.)
DAN	I've lost her. (Moves across front of auditorium.)
	(PICKLES swings round and runs with DAFFY following to R. steps into auditorium. KING and QUEEN see DAFFY.)
KING & QUEEN	Daffy! (They rise and give chase into auditorium.)
	(PICKLES moves across front after DAN. DAFFY runs up R. aisle and out through exit at end with KING and

	THE SLEEPING BEAUTY

QUEEN following giving suitable pursuing cries. DAN moves onstage over L. steps, PICKLES follows and both run off L. onstage. JENNY enters through pass door L.)

JENNY   Now where am I?   (Moving onstage over L. steps.) Anyway, now's me chance to get me spinning wheel. (Retrieves case from behind dais and moves to go into audience again.)   I wonder if this leads to the topmost whatsit?

(KING and QUEEN appear at L. back of auditorium.)

Ooh, no.   (Runs off L. onstage.)

KING & QUEEN   Daffy! Daffy!

KING   No, he's not here.

(DAFFY runs back through R. exit door.)

There he is!

(Runs across rear transverse aisle and after DAFFY as he runs down R. aisle.)

QUEEN   (running down L. aisle)   I'll head him off this way!

(DAFFY runs onstage over R. steps followed by KING. QUEEN returns over L. steps and between them they manage to capture DAFFY. HOUSE OUT.)

Oh, he loves a good run, don't you, Daffy?

DAFFY   (nods happily)

QUEEN   You do too, don't you, dear?

(KING panting heavily nods weakly. QUEEN kneels beside DAFFY.)

Now, we want you to do a little something for us, Daffy love.   (To KING.)   Get the boiler, dear.

(KING does so.)

(To DAFFY.)   Just boil up some water.   (To KING.)   Right, pop it over, ducks.

(KING cannot see clearly what he is doing and starts to pop it over QUEEN.)

Sc. 3   THE SLEEPING BEAUTY   61

	Not over me!
	(KING gets it off her and together they get it over DAFFY.)
	Tuck his tail in. That's it. (Shouting to DAFFY inside.) You don't mind – (Sees a tube sticking out and speaks down it.) You don't mind, do you, Daffy?
	(Severe agitation from boiler, they have to hold it down.)
KING	I think he does. (Peering through another pipe.) He's fuming in there.
QUEEN	Ah well, he'll get the water boiled all the quicker.
ROUND	(off R.) Render, where are you?
RENDER	(off L.) Coming, Sir Round.
KING	Quick, hide again!
	(Both get behind trolley. ROUND enters R. as RENDER enters L., also in full armour and with a lance, but groping like a blind man because he has his helmet on back to front.)
ROUND	Ah, there you are.
RENDER	Am I? I can't see where I am at all.
ROUND	Don't fuss over unimportant details, Render. If you're to win the Princess's hand you must do well in the joust; so we'll start with the tilt simple – otherwise known as a simple tilt. Right, you're over there, I'm over here – tilt.
	(RENDER leans over.)
	Not that sort of tilt. I want you to charge me – and don't you dare say how much. Right – charge!
	(RENDER raises lance and charges straight at AUDIENCE.)
	Stop!
	(RENDER stops at very edge of stage.)

	My dear boy, I just saved you.
RENDER	Really? Thanks awfully!
ROUND	Not at all. You nearly severely damaged an innocent bystander, well, bysitter really. Now, can you see at all?
RENDER	Yes, through my left earhole.
ROUND	Really? You must see an eye specialist.
RENDER	I mean I can see a little bit through the vent hole.
ROUND	Well, that's good enough. I'm the big steel thing over here. Charge me.
RENDER	The big steel thing. Righto.
	(He charges full tilt at boiler. As he strikes it simultaneous FLASH. EFFECT 10.MAROON off R. and BLACKOUT. Shouts and cries, clatter of falling armour as dummy empty suit of armour is put on. RENDER exits R. KING and QUEEN pull trolley upstage. LIGHTS UP to reveal QUEEN lying in front of trolley, KING over it, RENDER's apparently prone form, DAFFY looking rather dazed with his head out of the top of boiler and its lid perched like a wide-brimmed rather saucy hat on his head and ROUND knocked out and sitting on floor against a wing. PRINCESS rushes on L.)
PRINCESS	What's the matter? What's happened?
PICKLES	(running on R.) Stand back! Stand back! Is the Princess safe? Oh, thank goodness. (Faints.)
QUEEN	(sitting up and shaking head) Ooh. Is the tea ready? (Sees KING and jumps up.) Archibald! Archibald!
KING	(looking up) It's all right, my dear, don't worry. The buns are quite safe. (Rises and reveals that he has been lying over them.) Squashed but quite safe.
PRINCESS	(moving to PICKLES) Jester! Jester! Oh, do come round, I'm quite all right. (Helps him to

Sc. 3   THE SLEEPING BEAUTY

sit up.)

PICKLES   Where am I? Where am I?   (Sees PRINCESS.)
          Ah, in heaven.   (Faints again.)

ROUND   (coming round and seeing RENDER's prone form)
          Render! Render, are you all right? Speak to me,
          Render. He doesn't answer!

QUEEN   Perhaps he's not in. Give him a knock.

ROUND   (knocking on armour)   Render, are you there?
          (Tries to open helmet and it comes off in his hand.)
          Aah! He's been beheaded!   (Holds up helmet.)
          Alas, poor Render.   (Starts to sniffle.)   Like a
          son to me, you know. Ah, Render, if only you were
          still here.

RENDER   (poking head on R.)   I am. I got blown out.
          (He enters R., shamefacedly clutching his underwear
          about him.)

          (MUSIC 43.   Enter DAN R.)

DAN   The suitors are just coming over the drawbridge, Your
          Majesty.

KING   What! Then get all this stuff away! Raise the
          portcullis! Quickly, everybody!

          (DAN moves to raise portcullis. RENDER takes empty
          suit of armour off R., helped by ROUND who then
          returns. DAFFY lifts boiler by handles inside and runs
          off R. in it. KING and QUEEN push trolley off L.
          and return to seat themselves on dais. During all the
          bustle PRINCESS gently lays PICKLES down.)

PRINCESS Well, I shall sneak off on my own. What do I care
          now for all the suitors in the world?   (She exits L.)

          (DAFFY returns and sniffs at PICKLES.)

PICKLES   (sitting up)   Ah, Princess, Princess!   (Is about
          to embrace DAFFY then opens his eyes.)   Aah!

DAN   Her Royal Highness's Suitors!

          (MUSIC 44.   CHORUS enter through portcullis as
          Suitors and Attendants. They bow to KING and

	QUEEN.)
KING	Welcome! Let the joust commence!
	(EFFECT 11. Loud clap of thunder, Lightning. EFFECT 12. Wind.)
QUEEN	Ah, typical garden party weather.
	(DIM LIGHTS. EFFECT 13. More lightning and thunder. Start rain projector - a torrential downpour. CHORUS and PICKLES huddle D.S. miserably. ROUND draws his sword which turns out to be an umbrella and puts it up.)
ROUND	Don't worry, ma'am, I'm prepared for anything!
	(EFFECT 14. Sudden squall of wind. His umbrella blows inside out. Canopy collapses on their Majesties. Lines operated by KING and QUEEN.
	BLACKOUT.
	Close traverse tabs, fly in turret cloth and set truck. LIGHTS UP.)
	MUSIC 45. "RAIN, RAIN"
CHORUS	Drip, drop, pitter, patter, Splish, splash, POUR!
PICKLES	That's the way it goes on a typical day In a typical month from June to May.
CHORUS	Flick, flick, rumble, rumble, Crash, bang, ROAR!
PICKLES	That's the weather running true to form With a typical English thunderstorm.
ALL	Washed out girls and fellers;
PICKLES	Blown-out umbrellas; Such days, even on Sundays,
CHORUS	We get drenched right through our undays!
ALL	Pelt, pelt, buckets, torrents - Here it comes again. It's a habit shared,

Sc. 4   THE SLEEPING BEAUTY   65

>We are never prepared
>Whenever it starts to rain.

(Dance.)

>Rain, rain, rain, rain, rain!

(BLACKOUT. All exit. Open traverse tabs.)

Scene 4   The Topmost Turret of the Tallest Tower

Three-quarter set. Cloth showing battlements at top of a tower. In front of it L., a truck on the onstage end of which is a small spiral staircase rising to a door which opens onto the upper platform. This has a backing to represent a little turret room, with a small window in it which has a bar in the centre. There is room for a person behind this backing. Small stool set on platform. (If the use of a truck is impractical set on stage level.)

MUSIC 46. We see a tiny CARABOSSE outside the window flying towards it. (A glove puppet worked by CARABOSSE herself behind backing.)

CARABOSSE (voice)   Ah, here's the window. Hey, watch out! (Crashes into window bar then clutches onto it with one arm and rubs papier mache nose with other.)
This bar on purpose hit my snout.

(MUSIC 47   as she waves one arm.)

>Now, by my pow'rs supercharg'd,
>I bid myself – be thou enlarg'd!

(BLACKOUT. FLASH. CARABOSSE come from behind backing. Shouts of dismay from her. LIGHTS UP to reveal her struggling on floor with one foot stuck in window. She wears a long cloak.)

>Just look at that, the silly spell
>Has gone and work'd too quick, too well!

	Come out, you pesky foot, come free, For soon the Princess here might be. Before I left I set in motion My newt and zither luring potion. Like this I'd look a fool I feel. Come to that, I've no spinning wheel! (Enter JENNY R., carrying case containing spinning wheel.)
JENNY	Whew! This is the tallest tower, all right. My legs are killing me. They ought to hurry up and invent lifts. That must be the topmost turret. (Crosses.) * More stairs. Ah well. (Climbs them.) * (* * Cut between asterisks if a truck is not used.)
CARABOSSE	(wrenches foot free) Ah, at last! (Rubs foot.) Ooh, it does feel sore. (JENNY taps at door.) Just in time someone at the door. (Hobbles across and opens it cautiously.) Ah, glad to see you, that's a fact. Come in, let's get the wheel unpack'd. (She starts to do so with eager haste.)
JENNY	All right, but take it easy now, That spindle's sharp and you might – ow! Well there, I have, I've prick'd my – (Sucks finger.)
CARABOSSE	No! Then now you'll – Oh my goodness – oh! Quick think – some antidote or balm, Some antitoxic occult charm – Ah, I know! I'll exorcise it! No, I shan't! I'll cauterise it! No, I can't! 'Tis dire dread disaster! Oh, for a magic sticking plaster!
JENNY	Garn! I've 'ad worse than this before, 'Tain't worth your fussing so, I'm sure.
CARABOSSE	Ah, she can't guess her dreadful fate.

Sc. 4 THE SLEEPING BEAUTY

	Alas, my dear, that spindle's – wait!
	It isn't – yet! I am a nit,
	I've still to cast my spell on it.
	(Grabs JENNY's finger.)
	Pooh, pooh, a scratch, 'twill soon be gone.
JENNY	That's what I –
CARABOSSE	Now, don't carry on.
	I've things to do, so off you go.
JENNY	Hold on a jiff. You're sure you know
	How to make this spinning wheel work?
CARABOSSE	(crosses to door and indicates for JENNY to go)
	Yes, yes, of course.
JENNY	It's got a quirk.
CARABOSSE	(abstractedly looking around outside door)
	How nice.
JENNY	It's not. It's most perverse;
	The fly-wheel twirls, but in reverse.
	So lots of tension's what you need.
CARABOSSE	I have. (Moves to her.)
JENNY	That's this knob.
CARABOSSE	(leading her to door) Yes, indeed.
JENNY	(stopping as CARABOSSE tries to push her through)
	But not too much or else the thread'll
	Get tangled when you start to treadle.
	(Goes, shutting door.)
CARABOSSE	At last!
JENNY	(opening door) Goodbye.
CARABOSSE	Good riddance!
JENNY	Eh?
CARABOSSE	Goodbye to you, I meant to say.
JENNY	(going down steps and crossing R.)
	Queer old bird. Still mustn't mock 'er,
	It seems to me she's off her rocker. (Exits R.)

(CARABOSSE takes off her cloak and drapes it over spinning wheel case and reveals herself disguised as a comfortable old body.)

CARABOSSE   There, a disguise that's apt and canny,
To make me look a spinning granny.
Now, little spindle, listen well,
While I prepare thee with my spell.

(MUSIC 48. and LIGHTS DIM. As she speaks spindle tip glows (switch on spinning wheel operated by CARABOSSE with her foot).)

With venom vile I thee endow,
Sharp as a serpent's tooth be thou,
To bite the Princess and bite deep
And bring her everlasting sleep!
(She ends with a cackle of laughter, which she breaks off suddenly.)
Something innocent this way comes —
So this old granny spins and hums.

(She sits on stool spinning and humming innocuously as PRINCESS enters R. with her Dreamdust phial which she unstoppers and shakes.)

PRINCESS   Not a grain, not a granule. Never mind, I still have my dream.   (Looks around.)   I've never been to the top of this tower before. And there's another little turret to it yet. I must explore up* there.
(* change to "in" if truck is not used.)

(CARABOSSE rubs hands expectantly as PRINCESS starts to climb stairs. She stops.)

Or should I? No, I ought to get back, really.

(CARABOSSE looks despairing as she descends.)

But still, I would like to know what's through that little door.

(LIGHTS FADE as she climbs, CARABOSSE sniggers. Close traverse tabs.   MUSIC 49.)

Sc. 5   THE SLEEPING BEAUTY   69

Scene 5   A Corridor in the Palace

Tabs. CHORUS discovered, still as Suitors etc., but wrapped in towels and DAN administering to them from some medicine bottles with a large spoon.

MUSIC 50.   "COUGH AD SDEEZE!"

CHORUS
It's cold edough for sdowig;
A bitter widd is blowig;
   We thikk we're gettig chilblaids od our dees.
Id this eterdal drizzle
We're odly fit to grizzle
   Ad sdeeze ad cough ad sdeeze ad cough ad sdeeze.
     We feel blue -
     At-CHOO!
There's dot a side of ever leavig off.
We've really lost our grip,
We just stadd aroudd ad drip
   Ad cough ad sdeeze ad cough ad sdeeze ad cough.

DAN
I hope it won't distress you
If I stop saying, "Bless you!"
   It seems your germs a solid hold have got.
In vain I've tried to reach 'em
With powders made by Beecham
   And aspirin and linctus and the lot.
     Oh, my!
     Still not dry!
You're an awful lot of miseries to see.
I've bought ev'rything that's sold
For the curing of your cold,
   But dow I thikk you've gived it to be!

DAN & CHORUS
   We're croakig ad we're wheezig ev'rythig.
It's been goig od so log
We bust edd this little sog,
   'Cos we're fideig it ibpossible to sig, to sig,
   We're fideig it ibpos -   (They finish mouthing and exit L.)

THE SLEEPING BEAUTY   Part I

(EFFECT 15. A curious clanking sound off R. and SIR ROUND, the apparent cause of it, enters still in his armour moving like a clumsy robot with rigid arms and legs.)

ROUND   Render! Render! Blow that umbrella blowin' inside out. Now me armour's all rusted up. Still, a drop of oil should put that right. Render! I can't wear me other set; the Blacksmith sent it back with two left legs. Deuced awkward, I have to ride side saddle in it. Render, where's that oil?

(SIR RENDER enters R. with large oil can.)

RENDER   Here it is, Sir Round. Are you sure you want it, though?

ROUND   Of course.   (Nods very emphatically so that his visor falls down.)

RENDER   It doesn't look awfully nice.

(Noises from ROUND inside helmet.)

(Raising voice.)   What's that? I can't hear, your visor's fallen down.

(ROUND indicates that he is aware of that.)

Well, why don't you put it up?

(ROUND demonstrates his inability to bend his arms.)

I say, I do believe your armour's got rusty. Well, I'll do it for you.   (Tries to raise visor.)   I can't. That's jolly bad luck. I don't think there's anything we can do about it.

(Noises from ROUND.)

A can opener? From the kitchen, you mean?

(More noises.)

Oh, the oil can. Well, of course, I'll give you some if you really want it.   (Pokes the spout of oil can into a visor vent and squirts it.)   Here you –

(ROUND brings a rigid arm round to clonk RENDER.)

Sc. 5 THE SLEEPING BEAUTY

RENDER What's the - ?

(A rigid leg comes up and kicks him.)

Hey, look - Ow!

(The other one kicks him and they exit L. continuing the process. Enter PICKLES R., in a properly fitting jester's costume.)

PICKLES (sneezing) I think I must have caught pneumonia in that storm. Oh well, I've had it before. Ooh, I think there's a joke there. I've had pneumonia before so it wouldn't be - I'm on the verge - it wouldn't be - I'll get it in a minute - (Sneezes.) I've lost it. Still, at least getting drenched has shrunk my costume so it fits me better. In fact, the shoes are a bit too tight. (Bends to ease toes. <u>EFFECT 16. Loud splitting sound.</u> He freezes in mid bend, clutching his rear.) So are my tights too tight. I'll nip up to my room and carry out a running repair. Pity about that joke, though. It's only the funny bit that's missing. Pneumonia? Had it before so it's - ah, of course - it's - (Sneezes.) It's gone again. (Sneezes violently. <u>EFFECT 17. More ripping sound.</u>) Ooh, I'll have to go, too. It's getting draughty. (He almost turns his back, but hurriedly faces AUDIENCE again and sidles off L.)

(<u>MUSIC 51.</u> Boa 4 appears on R. arch. AUDIENCE shout. QUEEN looks on D.L.)

QUEEN Oh dear, how awkward. We're trying to dry out our clothes. Well, you must promise not to look. (She darts on and runs across to R. in her underwear.)

(Boa comes out more as she does so.)

Fluffy, you're peeking. Still it makes it easier for me to -

(Boa shoots out of sight with a siren whizz as she reaches for it.)

Ooh, how aggravating. I could have just done with it now to help cover me up till we get our clothes dry.

	(Calling off.) How are they getting on, Archibald?
	(KING enters L., also in his underwear, carrying a clothes horse draped with some garments. He hurriedly wraps clothes horse round himself when he realises AUDIENCE.)
KING	Ooh, you should have told me we had company, my dear.
QUEEN	It's all right, love, they're all members of a new society.
KING	What's that?
QUEEN	The permissive society.
KING	Oh, very topical, my dear. (Starts to weep.) Most witty, extremely humorous.
QUEEN	Well, don't enjoy it too much, love, or you'll get the clothes wetter than ever. Are they coming along all right?
KING	(feeling them) They're not quite dry. (Wrings out a sopping garment.)
QUEEN	We'll have to think of something.
	(ENTER DAFFY R.)
	Ah, Daffy, love - of course.
DAFFY	(shakes himself like a dog)
QUEEN	Oh, poor thing, you got caught in the storm too, didn't you?
DAFFY	(nods miserably)
QUEEN	Never mind, you won't mind giving us a hand, will you?
DAFFY	(nods emphatically and starts to run off R.)
QUEEN	No, no, dear - no more boilers. Just a bit of fire breathing to dry our clothes. You can do that, can't you?
DAFFY	(shakes head)

THE SLEEPING BEAUTY

QUEEN Of course you can. Go on, love.

DAFFY (shrugs, huffs and puffs and squirts a stream of water from his nostrils onto clothes)

QUEEN Oh dear, you did get wet, didn't you? Now what are we to do?

KING Ah! Wind!

QUEEN Have you, dear? It must have been those buns. Too much bicarb in them, I expect.

KING No, no, wind to dry the clothes. Let's blow on them.

QUEEN We can try it. Right - one, two, three - blow!

(All three blow. KING and QUEEN feel clothes.)

No, there's not enough of us to make a really good drying breeze. We must think again.

(All assume identical thinking positions. DAFFY is suddenly struck by an idea.)

He's thunked.

DAFFY (nods enthusiastically and points at AUDIENCE)

QUEEN What a novel notion. Clever Daffy.   (To AUDIENCE.)   Would you give us a good blow? You would? Well, wait till I say "blow" and then blow as hard as you can. If your teeth are a bit loose I should take them out. Well, you never know. Right - deep breath, hold it - blow!

(AUDIENCE blows.)

Dear, dear, bit short of puff, aren't we? Too much Christmas pud? Let's try again. Deep breath, hold it - blow!

(AUDIENCE blows.)

How are they doing, Archibald?

KING (feeling clothes)   Nearly dry. One more large exhalation should prove effective.

QUEEN One more - yes, well never mind that, just blow. Last time so take a very, very, very, very, very deep breath, hold it - blow!

(KING, QUEEN and DAFFY are all blown over, knocking over the clothes horse. Pull back and flap traverse tabs as if blown by a strong wind. Enter DAN L.)

DAN Are your Majesties ready to receive her Highness's suitors?

(All jump up. KING grabs first garment which comes to hand, which is the QUEEN's dress, and starts cramming it on assuming the sleeves to be trouser legs, while QUEEN searches for it in the remaining clothes with DAFFY's help.)

KING What! The suitors!

DAN Yes, I've managed to dry them out now, sire.

QUEEN My dress - where's my dress?

KING Well, of course we're not ready to receive them. Can't you see?

QUEEN (flinging garments all over DAFFY) It must be here somewhere.

KING I think these trousers have shrunk.

QUEEN Oh, Archibald, really. You've got it.

KING What? Oh sorry, my love. (Takes it off.) Well, give us half a moment, Chamberlain, and then summon the court. And, of course, the Princess. Where is she, by the way? Come to think of it, I haven't seen her for some time.

DAN Nor have I, Your Majesty.

QUEEN Nor me. How about you, Daffy?

DAFFY (shakes head)

KING Well, I wonder where she is?

(FADE LIGHTS. All exit. MUSIC 52. Open traverse tabs.)

Scene 6   The Topmost Turret

Scene as before. FADE UP LIGHTS. PRINCESS at top of steps about to open door, CARABOSSE at wheel.

PRINCESS There may be someone in here. I'd better knock. (Taps at door.)

CARABOSSE At last! At last! My triumph's nigh!
She's bound to ask if she might try
To work the wheel, for 'tis quite sure
She's never seen its like before.

(PRINCESS taps a little louder. CARABOSSE assumes an old and pleasant voice.)

Come in, pray, whoever you be.

(PRINCESS opens door.)

A pretty sight my old eyes see.
Prithee step this way, my dear.

(She spins away very ostentatiously as PRINCESS comes in.)

PRINCESS Thank you. I've never been in here.

CARABOSSE Aye – twist the yarn – that's true, I'm sure.
Treadle the wheel and twist once more.

PRINCESS It's very small.

CARABOSSE Well, that's true too.
But not too small for what I do.
Twist, treadle and twist yet again.

PRINCESS And very high.

CARABOSSE Aye, 'tis, but then –
The flax works better at a height!
Treadle and twist all day and night.

PRINCESS The view's nice, though.

CARABOSSE Is it? Oh, aye,
I work too hard such things to spy.
<u>Twist</u>! <u>Treadle</u>!   (Aside.)   Will she never ask?

PRINCESS		I say, that seems a most strange task. Well, that sounds rude, I just meant though, What is – (Drops phial and it breaks.) My precious phial – oh no! From these sad fragments my dream grew. I pray my dream's not shatter'd too. (She starts to go.)
CARABOSSE		Going? (Aside.) My plans then go to ruin! Stay, you've not ask'd me what I'm doin'.
PRINCESS		I think 'twere best I should depart, I feel foreboding in my heart.
CARABOSSE		(aside) Stop her I must! But how? That's it! With me pathetic acting bit. (Very over pathetic and weepy.) Stay with a poor old crone awhile, My flagging spirits you'll beguile. Up here I don't see many folk, To laugh and talk and share a joke, For all my life is in my work, My spinning, which I never shirk.
PRINCESS		What is spinning?
CARABOSSE		'Tis how my dear, Raw wool or flax by this wheel here Into a single thread is spun.
PRINCESS		How clever and it looks such fun. Is it hard?
CARABOSSE		As easy as pie.
PRINCESS		I wonder?
CARABOSSE		(eagerly) Yes?
PRINCESS		Well, could I try?
CARABOSSE		(hastily rising) Of course, my pretty, here's the stool. (Aside, as PRINCESS sits.) She's caught at last, the little fool!

Sc. 6   THE SLEEPING BEAUTY

	Now twist the yarn, treadle the wheel –
	(PRINCESS starts spinning. <u>MUSIC 53.</u> Start to FADE LIGHTS.)
	Yes, that's it, you'll soon get the feel.
PRINCESS	It is easy, so peaceful too, (Operates foot switch to make spindle glow.) A gentle – (Pricks finger. Music sting.) Aah!
CARABOSSE	What did you do?
PRINCESS	'Tis nothing.
CARABOSSE	You never can tell. (Aside.) Bravo, spindle, you've work'd right well. For safety's sake you'd better go And to your parents this wound show.
PRINCESS	If you wish, but this will soon heal. (Sighs.) Pity too, I'd just got the feel. (Goes slowly through door shutting it.)
CARABOSSE	Oh yes, you got the feel all right, A feel to bring ne'er ending night! (As she starts to laugh pull truck off L. to leave stairs only in view with PRINCESS slowly descending them. Enter PICKLES R. Start to close traverse tabs slowly when PRINCESS is clear of steps. Fly out Turret cloth. Strike truck. Set for following scene.)
PICKLES	Ooh, the Princess! What a bit of luck I've just sewn myself in a gusset. But I must control myself. I musn't faint this time.
PRINCESS	Ah, Jester, I – I – (Starts to sway.)
PICKLES	I think she's going to. (Hastens across to hold her up.) It's my charm, of course, my fatal – fatal! (Seriously alarmed.) Princess, what is it? What's the matter?
PRINCESS	(very faintly) Nothing – I just – pricked my finger on – on – (Falls into PICKLES's arms.)

	(FADE LIGHTS to a single spot on them.)
PICKLES	Your finger! Oh, my Princess, I've failed you. Failed my lovely Princess.
	(BLACKOUT. <u>MUSIC 54.</u>)

Scene 7   The Royal Palace

Set as in Scene 1, but without the spinning wheels. Traverse tabs still drawn to begin.

Open in BLACKOUT. Voices heard first on one side then another calling for the PRINCESS, singly and far off at first then growing in number and volume and drawing nearer. LIGHT FADE UP and KING enters agitatedly L.

KING	Oh, where is she? Where is my daughter?
	(Enter DAN hurriedly R.)
DAN	No sign of her, sire.
	(1st CHORUS enters L. All when they enter are servants.)
1st CHORUS	She's not in her chamber.
	(2nd CHORUS enters L.)
2nd CHORUS	Not in her tiring room.
	(3rd and 4th CHORUS enter R.)
3rd & 4th CHORUS	Her drawing room.
	(ROUND enters L.)
ROUND	The courtyard.
	(RENDER enters R.)
RENDER	The garden.
	(QUEEN enters L.)

QUEEN	The kitchen.
	(DAFFY enters R. and shakes head.)
	And not in the dragonry either.
	(Open traverse tabs.)
KING	Then where is she? Where is the Princess?
	(JENNY enters U.L.)
JENNY	In the topmost turret of the tallest tower.
KING	The topmost turret –
QUEEN	Of the tallest tower?
BOTH	Why?
JENNY	Ah, it's a surprise.
KING	Who is this girl?
DAN	She's mine – I mean, my choice for the Maid of Honour.
JENNY	Yes, but I'm also – Well, that's part of the surprise.
KING & QUEEN	What surprise?
JENNY	Well, you'll know soon enough, so I might as well say. She's –
	(ALL move up a step towards her.)
	But don't get huffy 'cos they're new to you – She's learnin' –
	(ALL move up another step.)
	They're wonderfully handy and save lots of time – She's learnin' to –
	(ALL move up one more step.)
	Well, I brought it here so I know you'll be ever so pleased that she's learnt. Aren't you now?
ALL	(moving in a final step) Learnt what?
JENNY	Oh, didn't I say? Why, 'ow to spin with a spinnin' wheel.
	(ALL gasp and step back. Stunned silence.)

Coo, 'asn't it gone quiet?

QUEEN   Our child! We must save our child!

KING   Yes! Save the Princess! To the topmost tower!

ALL   To the topmost tower!

(ALL surge U.L., then stop suddenly and part, backing slowly away to make a pathway for PICKLES who enters with the PRINCESS in his arms. <u>MUSIC 55.</u>)

DAN   Quickly, a couch.

(CHORUS exit R.)

KING   It's – it's happened?

(PICKLES nods in dumb misery.)

QUEEN   Is she – ?

PICKLES   Not yet – not quite.

(CHORUS return with couch to R.C., and PICKLES lays PRINCESS gently on it.)

KING   Arrest that girl!

(CHAMPIONS take JENNY by each arm.)

DAN   But, sire –

KING   Silence! It's all her fault. To the dungeons with her!

JENNY   What me? What 'ave I done? What's the matter?

KING   Can't you see? The Princess has – has –

(CARABOSSE appears suddenly U.L. ALL hastily move away from her.)

CARABOSSE   Has courted death upon a spindle,
Just as I vow'd.

JENNY   Cor, what a swindle!
Why, you told me –

CARABOSSE   A pack of lies,
To gain my end, her swift demise.

(PRINCESS stirs a little.)

Sc. 7   THE SLEEPING BEAUTY

QUEEN   But she's not dead! Quick, save our daughter,
            Bring smelling salts!
DAN   A fan!
RENDER   Some water!
KING   Feathers for burning!
ROUND   Lots of brandy!
QUEEN   Sal Volatile if it's handy!
            (CHORUS rush to and fro during above and now exit.)
CARABOSSE   (laughing)
            Poor fools! No matter what you try,
            Your fair Princess will surely –
            (Enter DREAMAWHILE U.C. through double doors.)
DREAMAWHILE   Fie!
            You know she won't, you boastful thing.
            (Yawns.)
            Dear me, how sleep's last traces cling.
            Sorry I spoilt your climax, though,
            But you'll another find I know.
            Meanwhile I shall –
CARABOSSE   Just go and stew!
            You know there's nothing you can do.
DREAMAWHILE Of course there isn't.
            (Consternation.)
                            Not a one.
            (More consternation.)
            For all there is to do is done.
CARABOSSE   Too much sleep has soften'd your brain.
DREAMAWHILE (comfortingly)
            Ah. I'll in easy words explain.
            Did I not give this child a dream?
CARABOSSE   Yes, yes, of love, or some such scheme;
            So that she's had.

DREAMAWHILE	Don't be too swift, Her dream was only half my gift; Also it shall come true, said I. It hasn't - yet, so she can't die.
CARABOSSE	But my spell -
DREAMAWHILE	Cannot mine revoke! To quote some words you haply spoke.
CARABOSSE	What, what? But, but! No, no! You skunk! My dreamboat you have gone and sunk. (Crosses L. and turns.) But just you wait, I've still, I say A dirty trick or two to play! (She stumps off L.)
KING & QUEEN	Bravo!
DAN & CHAMPS	Well done!
KING	We always knew We could, of course, rely on you.
DREAMAWHILE	You did? Yes, well, a pleasant fiction Does help avoid unpleasant friction.
PICKLES	But wait, the Princess still lies here.
DREAMAWHILE	I know, don't worry, Pickles dear, Thus she'll lie in blissful sleep Till she her date with love can keep. (Waves wand.)

(LIGHTS FADE. Gauze panel R. of doors LIGHTS UP and the PRINCE is seen. The PRINCESS stirs slightly and smiles as he sings.)

MUSIC 56.   "YOU'LL SEE"   Reprise

PRINCE	Dream till the moment when your love is born, Dream till the perfumed magic of the dawn. Some day love will open your eyes And then with ecstasy and wonder and surprise - You'll see! You'll see! You'll see!

(FADE gauze LIGHTS and FADE UP scene LIGHTS.)

Sc. 7   THE SLEEPING BEAUTY   83

DREAMAWHILE   She shall sleep for a hundred years.
KING   A hundred!
QUEEN   No, no!
DREAMAWHILE   Calm your fears,
               'Tis four score till her Prince is born,
               And that she may not wake forlorn
               I'll send all you to sleep as well.

               (LIGHTS FADE. MUSIC 57. There is a music ting
               each time she points her wand. When she does who-
               ever is concerned falls to sleep immediately in whatever
               position they happen to be.)

               Two.   (KING and QUEEN.)
                    Three.   (DAN.)
                         Six.   (CHAMPIONS and JENNY.)
                              Seven.   (PICKLES.)
                                   In one spell.

DAFFY   (whinnies, not wanting to be left out)

DREAMAWHILE   Ah, Daffy dear, I had forgot.
               (She deals with him.)

               (MUSIC 58 sounds softly and Boa 4 appears on R. pros
               arch. FAIRY smiles and points wand, tune becomes
               very sleepy and Boa flops.)

               Now really that must be the lot.
               (Moves to PRINCESS and waves wand over her.)
               Sleep! Naught shall wake thee from thy bliss
               Till thy true Prince brings love's first kiss.
               (She exits R.)

               (LIGHTS now very low. Pause. MUSIC 59 and
               CARABOSSE enters stealthily L.)

CARABOSSE   But ere a Prince can stir thy slumber
               I shall the castle walls encumber
               With such a monstrous hedge of thorn
               'Twill stay all men of women born!

               (CHORUS enter as each Hedge Spirit is named.
               MUSIC 60.)

Come Hawthorn! Blackthorn! Thorn of Fire!
Come Bramble Bush! Come Thistle! Briar!
Weave tight that none dare penetrate in here
Not in a hundred, nay, a thousand year!

(Ballet led by CARABOSSE to represent building of hedge round castle with as many lavish effects as possible.)

CURTAIN

MUSIC 61. ENTR'ACTE

PART II

Scene 8   Dreamland

A very open scene. A cloud projector plays on the
cyc., sending light clouds slowly across it. Wings L.
and R. which should be a pretty design rather than
representing anything specific. In each is a delicately
framed gauze panel. A large but graceful stone urn
labelled "DREAMS" is C., and a prettily decorated
stand like a lectern D.R. BLACKOUT to open, which
is broken by a large electric sign suspended from Flies
flashing the word "DREAMLAND". FADE UP LIGHTS
for MUSIC 62. Ballet with CHORUS as Fairies led
by DREAMAWHILE. The CHORUS finish grouped in
pretty poses round her in which they nod off gracefully
as she speaks. MUSIC 63.

DREAMAWHILE   Behold my realm, my land of dreams,
Where thoughts are mountains, wishes streams;
Where nothing is and yet there's all;
Where hopes can rise to castles tall -
Castles in Spain or in the air.
This is a land all know and share.
Dreams though are as butterfly's wings,
Beautiful but most fragile things.
So lest one's broke - so eas'ly done -
Dream Guardians watch o'er ev'ryone
With ceaseless vigilance.   (Sees them asleep.)
                               Oh dear,
The air's so enervating here,
I'm half asleep myself.
(Shakes herself and gives a vigorous wave of her wand.)
                    Awake!

	(CHORUS are startled awake.)
	Our dream invent'ry let us take.
CHORUS	Yes, Ma'am!
	(1st and 2nd FAIRIES run to urn and 3rd, 4th, 5th and 6th run off R. 3rd and 4th return with a huge book labelled "DREAM REGISTER" which they put on stand; 5th with a very large quill pen and ink horn and 6th with a bag labelled "DREAM ADJUSTMENTS" and a large pair of spectacles which DREAMAWHILE puts on as she moves to consult Register.)
DREAMAWHILE	As years roll by apace Of ev'ry dream we must keep trace. We handle them with loving care, For each is but a globe of air.
	(1st and 2nd FAIRIES mime taking from urn what is evidently just such a thing and gently "throw" it up in front of gauze panel R.)
	Now see!
	(LIGHTS UP behind R. gauze and we see a tableau of the KING looking delightedly at a trolley bulging with rich goodies.)
	To guess an easy one. But put more currants in each bun, Then with the King all will be well. (She ticks book.)
	(FADE GAUZE LIGHTS. 5th and 6th FAIRIES mime taking "dream globe" and produce cartons labelled "CURRANTS" from bag and mime pouring them in before replacing "dream" in urn while the 3rd and 4th FAIRIES "take out" another "dream" and "throw" it up in front of gauze panel L. FADE UP LIGHTS behind it to reveal tableau of QUEEN proudly pointing at a poster announcing a massed choir concert to be conducted by Her Majesty Queen Coke in person.)
3rd FAIRY	Another simple one to tell.
DREAMAWHILE	Perhaps a little dusty though. (She makes a tick.)

Sc. 8   THE SLEEPING BEAUTY   87

(FADE GAUZE LIGHTS. 5th and 6th FAIRIES "take" it
and produce mini feather dusters from bag to dust it
then "replace" it in urn, while 1st and 2nd FAIRIES
"produce" the third "dream" and "throw" it up in front
of R. gauze. FADE UP GAUZE LIGHTS. A tableau
appears of DAFFY looking very fierce dragging away
one of CHORUS as a glamorous maiden in chains.
FAIRIES all laugh.)

A dream all dragons dream, I trow.

1st FAIRY   Daffy's damsel's in real distress,
                  Those chains are ruining her dress.

DREAMAWHILE   Loose them a mite.

(FADE GAUZE LIGHTS. DREAMAWHILE makes note
in book. 5th and 6th FAIRIES "take" "dream" to deal
with it and replace it in urn, while 3rd and 4th "take
out" and "throw up" 4th "dream" in front of L. panel.)

                         Rescue's at hand
In this shar'd dream.

(FADE UP L. GAUZE LIGHTS to show tableau of SIR
ROUND and SIR RENDER looking very valiant in
armour with St. George tabards of red crosses on white
grounds. SIR RENDER's is very long.)

                  A gallant band,

4th FAIRY   Any damsel they'd surely aid.

DREAMAWHILE   But see that tabard's shorter made.

(FADE GAUZE LIGHTS. She makes another note.
5th and 6th FAIRIES "take" it and 5th produces a pair
of scissors and 6th a needle and thread from bag to
make the required alteration before "returning" it to
urn. 1st COUPLE "take out" and "throw up" 5th
"globe" in front of R. panel.)

This too is shar'd.

2nd FAIRY   (sighing)   Each dreams of each.

(FADE UP R. GAUZE LIGHTS for tableau of JENNY
and DAN looking adoringly at each other.)

DREAMAWHILE	But please ensure, I do beseech, He has no little ling'ring thought Of other maids that once he sought.
	(FADE GAUZE LIGHTS. She makes mark in book. 5th and 6th FAIRIES "take" it and produce large magnifying glasses from bag to scrutinise it thoroughly. Evidently from the way they shake their heads there are indeed one or two such thoughts they have to "pluck out" before replacing it in urn. 3rd and 4th FAIRIES "take out" and "throw up" 6th "dream", in front of L. gauze.)
3rd FAIRY	Two dreams in one –
	(FADE UP L. GAUZE LIGHTS. We see a tableau of PICKLES smiling broadly with a cartoon balloon saying 'A JOKE' coming from the top of his head.)
DREAMAWHILE	That I shall grant His other though, alas, I can't.
	(PICKLES' smile turns to a soulful look as he reveals a large heart he has been clasping to himself on which is inscribed "PRINCESS" in bold letters.)
	'Tis hard to wrench a dream apart. Do it gently. Don't break his heart.
	(FADE GAUZE LIGHTS. With a sigh she makes a heavy deletion in her book. ALL FAIRIES "take" the "dream" sadly, and gently "pull" it apart before replacing it. DREAMAWHILE moves to urn.)
	But one more dream before we're done, The last and most important one. Is our sweet Beauty's dream intact? For soon her fiction will be fact.
	(She "takes" out and "throws up" a "dream" in front of R. gauze, FADE UP R. GAUZE LIGHTS. A tableau of the PRINCE appears. FADE SCENE LIGHTS. BRING UP SPOT L. where PRINCESS enters. Gradually FADE GAUZE LIGHTS during number.)

Sc. 8   THE SLEEPING BEAUTY

MUSIC 64.   "THE STUFF OF DREAMS"

PRINCESS
Here's the stuff of dreams –
'Tis the stardust in our eyes;
'Tis the magic of the moon slowly setting.
Here's the balm of sleep,
Sweet invader of the mind,
Tender guardian of our hopes,
And the gentle child that comes of sleep's
                               begetting.
Here my future I can see
As the pages of a book I am turning.
Here's the stuff of dreams,
All the hopes and loves and fears
With the passing of the years
All the passion in my heart forever burning.
Here's the stuff of dreams, the happiness and
                               yearning.

(FADE SPOT. Exit PRINCESS L. DREAMAWHILE "takes" down "dream".)

DREAMAWHILE   All's well, let's put the dreams away.

(As FAIRIES move to pick up urn FLASH and CARABOSSE leaps on L. MUSIC 65. Race clouds across cyc. CHORUS FAIRIES jump away and huddle together R.)

CARABOSSE
Yes, yes I should without delay –
What's left!
(Touches with her wand the "dream" "held" by DREAMAWHILE.)

(Popping noise, ORCHESTRA.)

         Ooh, how they do go pop!
(Runs to urn to deal with the other dreams.)

(Six popping noises.)

(As she runs off L.)
He-he! That caught you on the hop!

(Slow clouds to previous speed.)

DREAMAWHILE   (sighing a little impatiently)

	Sometimes, I fear, she does lack charm.
3 FAIRIES	Our dreams!
OTHER 3	What can we do?
DREAMAWHILE	Keep calm, And think how we can save this waste.
1st FAIRY	Dream glue, ma'am?
2nd FAIRY	Or fantasy paste?
3rd FAIRY	Reverie rivets?
4th FAIRY	Pipe dream plaster?
DREAMAWHILE	No, 'tis not that bad a disaster. (Looking in urn.) Some dreams are torn and some just mixed. I know how best to get them fix'd, I'll all the dreamers summon here Then each dream's fault will soon be clear. Away and have new dream globes made.

(FAIRIES flit off R. DREAMAWHILE waves wand. <u>MUSIC 66.</u>)

Dreamers, come hence, ere thy dreams fade.
(She backs off R.)

(The QUEEN enters L., dreamily.)

QUEEN	Now that's very odd, I had a lovely dream a minute ago and it suddenly went pop. It must be around somewhere.

(A large white balloon inscribed "DREAM" floats on from R.)

Ah, there's one.   (Catches it.)

(KING runs on R.)

KING	No, no that's my dream, my dear.

(PICKLES runs on L.)

PICKLES	No mine.
QUEEN	Well, let's share it.

Sc. 8 THE SLEEPING BEAUTY 91

        (MUSIC 67. Comic balloon dance ending with the balloon being burst between them.)

KING My dream! (Holding up a bit of burst balloon.) No, maybe it wasn't after all. (Wanders off R.)

PICKLES And come to think of it mine's a double dream. (Wanders off L.)

QUEEN Obviously just an idle dream. But I do wish I could find mine.

        (DAFFY enters R. He stops and looks at her quizzically.)

Oh, Daffy love, have you got a dream, dear?

DAFFY (nods)

QUEEN What is it?

DAFFY (gives a wild roar, makes a fierce lunge at QUEEN and starts to drag her off R.)

QUEEN Daffy! You silly thing, you're not a big, fierce dragon.

DAFFY (nods emphatically)

QUEEN What do you think I am then – a glamorous maiden?

DAFFY (scratches head puzzled for a moment then shrugs and nods)

QUEEN But I'm – well, maybe you're right.

        (SIR ROUND bounds on L.)

ROUND Dastardly dragon! Stop! Thank heavens I found our dream in time.

        (SIR RENDER bounds on R., in a shorter tabard.)

RENDER What's this – a damsel in distress! The honour's mine, dear lady.

ROUND Sir! Stand back, the honour's mine!

QUEEN Oh, I say, what lovely dreams people have. Do go on.

ROUND Just wait there, dragon, while we settle this. Point of honour, you know. (Draws sword.) Now, sir, will you give way?

RENDER	No, no, Sir Render will never surrender! Funny, that never struck me before.	
ROUND	Then fall to!	
RENDER	Eh? Oh very well. (Falls down, dropping sword.)	
ROUND	No, no, that means we start fightin'.	
RENDER	Does it?	
ROUND	Yes, like lay on.	
RENDER	Lay on? I thought he was a Chinese knight.	
ROUND	Stop yammering and start fightin'.	
RENDER	(rising holding sword wrong way round) Right, I'm ready. (Notices sword.) Almost. (He turns it round.)	
	(A rather static comic fight follows with each taking it in turn to strike a blow in which they are watched as at a tennis match by DAFFY and the QUEEN. The fight ends by their suddenly striking each other simultaneously and knocking each other out. DAFFY waggles his head happily and pulls QUEEN off R.)	
QUEEN	(as they go) Oh well.	
	(1st FAIRY runs on L. and 2nd on R. each with a towel with which they quickly fan each hero then help him up and off, RENDER to R. and ROUND to L. 3rd and 4th FAIRIES run squealing on from L. chased by DAN. MUSIC 68. DREAMAWHILE enters R. They run behind her. She puts up her wand which halts him, then she gives it a little twirl and points to L. where JENNY is just entering upstage. DAN swivels round and runs L. but they both run straight past each other and off on opposite sides. The 3 FAIRIES look at each other puzzled. The PRINCESS enters D.L.)	
PRINCESS	My love, my dream. Where is my dream love?	
	(DREAMAWHILE points with wand U.R. where PRINCE enters. Both run towards and straight past each other, then stop puzzled, PRINCE D.L. and PRINCESS U.R.	

Sc. 8 THE SLEEPING BEAUTY

	Their faces clear and both say –)
BOTH	My love.
	(– just as JENNY enters D.R. and DAN U.L. The PRINCE hastens R., but to JENNY and they clasp hands but look vaguely uncomfortable, while DAN and the PRINCESS meet L. similarly. <u>MUSIC 69</u> "CONFUSION!". During number DREAMAWHILE silently directs the 3rd and 4th FAIRIES to sort them out.)
PRINCE	I'm in love with a certain someone; Pray, who can it be?
JENNY	Now my brain has become a numb one; Is it him or he?
ALL	Help, help! What a sorry state When you can't find your mate.
PRINCESS	It seems I have mislaid a lover; Tell me, is it you?
DAN	We'll need a programme to discover Who's in love with who.
	(3rd and 4th FAIRIES move them round.)
ALL	Help, help! Nobody can guess The way out of this mess.
	(DAN and PRINCE land together and PRINCESS and JENNY. During following DREAMAWHILE indicates to FAIRIES that it is not right.)
PRINCE	Good day to you.
DAN	Good day to you.
BOTH	Are you the one I chose?
PRINCESS	Are you the one I dreamed about?
JENNY	Or is it one of those?
PRINCE & DAN	We're in love with a certain someone; Pray, who can it be?
PRINCESS & JENNY	Do you think that you could become one Who's in love with me?

THE SLEEPING BEAUTY — Part II

(3rd and 4th FAIRIES move them to their proper partners.)

ALL
    Help, help! What a sorry show
    When no one seems to know.

(DREAMAWHILE indicates that all is satisfactory and 3rd and 4th FAIRIES exit R.)

    Here at last is a solution;
    Here's a way from this confusion –
    Now I know that I'm the one in love with you!

(JENNY and DAN exit happily U.R. Just as the PRINCE and PRINCESS are going off, PICKLES enters D.R. <u>MUSIC 70.</u>)

PICKLES   Princess! My Princess! My dream –

(PRINCESS runs to PICKLES, smiles and squeezes his hand, then turns again to join her PRINCE and exit L. with him.)

My dream's gone wrong.

(DREAMAWHILE shakes her head sadly. PICKLES does likewise and moves slowly off U.R. DREAMAWHILE sighs and puts her hand out to R. where a book labelled "JOKES" is put into it and thumbing through it, she follows him off R. DAFFY returns from D.R. now dragging the QUEEN in chains. RENDER runs on after them with a large bandage round his head instead of his helmet, as ROUND runs on from L. similarly bandaged. The QUEEN makes herself prettily ready to be saved.)

ROUND & RENDER   Hold, vile dragon!   (They realise each other.)
Oh.

ROUND   After you.

RENDER   No, er – your seniority gives you precedence.

ROUND   Ah but, youth to the fore, what?

RENDER   Age must have its fling, or something like that.

ROUND   Sir, I insist.

Sc. 8 THE SLEEPING BEAUTY 95

RENDER Well, I jolly well do too.

(They continue to bow and scrape, but the QUEEN has grown impatient and moves R. while DAFFY is still staring fascinated.)

QUEEN Well, come on! (She gives a tug on chain and drags DAFFY off U.L.)

ROUND Tell you what, both together then.

(They turn in.)

BOTH They've gone! (They look off L.)

RENDER) Hey, wait! Come back!
) (Together)
ROUND) Stop, I say, stop!

BOTH (running off L.) Wait for us to save you!

(PICKLES enters D.R. backing away from 5th and 6th FAIRIES who are trying to thrust on him the trolley loaded with goodies, particularly buns and custard pies.)

PICKLES No, no. It's not my dream I tell you.

(FAIRIES nod their heads eagerly and push it in front of him.)

You've made a mistake. I don't like –

(5th FAIRY stuffs a cream bun into his mouth, 6th FAIRY plonks a custard pie in his hand, and they exit happily R.)

I'll never manage to eat all this. (Disconsolately chews on bun.) It's not right, you know, lumbering people with other people's dreams.

(Enter KING U.R.)

KING Not a sign of my dream. Not so much as a crumb – (Sees the trolley.) Ooh! I say, are you sure you've got the right dream?

PICKLES No, I'm not. It wasn't my idea at all. They insisted. Why, do you want some?

KING	Oh, no. No, not at all. I'm not hungry. (Starts to move away and suddenly turns back.) But since you insist I'll toy with a little something. (Grabs a large bun in each hand.)	
PICKLES	I mean, all I'm interested in is inventing a joke, and what joke is there to be found in – (He is about to take a bite of the custard pie he holds, but stops as a thought dawns on him. He looks at the KING, contentedly stuffing himself with gurgles of pleasure through his mouthfuls of bun. He looks back at the pie and weighs it thoughtfully in his hand. He looks quickly back at the KING then back to the pie and starts to giggle.)	
KING	Yes, you were saying?	
	(PICKLES laughs more.)	
	Don't just stand there giggling.	
PICKLES	(gasping through his laughter) But I – I've just thought of a joke.	
KING	Well, let's hear it then.	
PICKLES	(through bursts of laughter) A wonderful joke! The most wonderful joke in the world and I've invented it!	
KING	(exasperated) But what is it?	
PICKLES	(calming himself) I'm sorry. Well, you see this custard pie?	
KING	Yes, I see that custard pie.	
PICKLES	(has a fit of laughter and stops abruptly) That's the joke.	
KING	(thinks for a moment and shakes head) I must have missed a bit somewhere.	
PICKLES	(weighing the pie again) Oh, you won't miss any of this joke. (Has another burst of laughter and controls himself again.) Because – because I'm going to push this pie – (Laughs.)	
KING	Yes?	

Sc. 8 THE SLEEPING BEAUTY

PICKLES	I'm going to push this pie into – (Laughs.)
KING	Yes, yes?
PICKLES	Into your –
	(And just as he is about to suit the action to the word SIR RENDER enters and unwittingly bumps into him making him push the pie into his own face. This is not SIR RENDER's fault as, together with SIR ROUND and the QUEEN, he has been propelled on by DAFFY who now has them all enchained. The KING immediately bursts into tears at the joke.)
	(Wiping some pie off his face.) It doesn't seem so funny now.
KING	It does to me. (Cries more copiously.)
PICKLES	Well, maybe if – (He eyes SIR RENDER and picks up another pie.) Yes. Coo-ee!
	(SIR RENDER turns, but ducks and PICKLES gets ROUND. The KING weeps harder than ever.)
ROUND	I suppose you think that's funny. (He breaks his chains and strides over to the trolley where he selects a custard pie and buzzes it at PICKLES.)
	(PICKLES jumps back so that it hits the KING. It instantly stops his tears.)
KING	Treason! (He stumps furiously over to the trolley to sling one back at ROUND but misses and gets the QUEEN.)
QUEEN	(breaking her chains) Archibald! (She picks up a pie, but misses the KING and gets SIR RENDER.)
	(A free-for-all develops. DAFFY obviously feels left out of it and tries to get their attention. He picks up a pie and ALL back away from him, but he plonks it on himself and trots off L. happily. The pies all gone they start throwing buns (the cotton wool ones) first at each other and then to the AUDIENCE. At this point five outraged FAIRIES enter R. with five mops, which they thrust into their hands.)

KING	Oh dear, I suppose we have made rather a mess.
	(FAIRIES nod agreement grimly then turn haughtily and walk off. The five culprits start to mop up.)
PICKLES	Well, it all started as a joke.
RENDER	It was a jolly - jolly joke too.
ROUND	And a jolly old joke, but then -
CHAMPIONS) KING) QUEEN)	There's no jokes like the old jokes.
PICKLES	I don't wish to know that.

<u>MUSIC 71.</u>   "I DON'T WISH TO KNOW THAT"

	I don't wish to know that.
OTHERS	But old jokes are the rage.
PICKLES	I still don't wish to know that - Kindly leave the -
	(Music continues vamping under patter, which should be delivered very rapidly.)
QUEEN	But what about the one about my dog?
PICKLES	What about your dog?
QUEEN	He was in an accident. His nose was cut off.
PICKLES	Really? How does he smell?
QUEEN	Terrible! (Produces and puts on a red nose.)
PICKLES	I don't wish -
	(ROUND and RENDER put on red noses.)
RENDER	I say, I say, I say, I call my dog Sausage.
ROUND	Do you? Why?
RENDER	Because he's half bred.
KING	(putting on a red nose) I never "sausage" a thing. (Saw such.)
PICKLES	I don't wish to know that,

Sc. 8   THE SLEEPING BEAUTY

                           Your jokes all creak with age.

OTHERS   Well, that is why we know them.

PICKLES   Kindly leave the –

(Music continues vamping. Enter DAN R. with a red nose.)

DAN   I say, I say, I say, do you know what just happened in the park?

PICKLES   No, what just happened in the park?

DAN   There were two peanuts on a bench and one was a salted.

PICKLES   I don't wish –

(Enter JENNY R. with a red nose.)

JENNY   I say, I say, I say, what do you get if you cross peanut butter with an elephant?

PICKLES   I don't know. What do I get if I cross peanut butter with an elephant?

JENNY   Peanut butter with a long memory.

PICKLES   If you can get away with that so can I. (Puts on a red nose. To QUEEN.) I say, I say, I say, what do you get if you cross peanut butter with an elephant?

QUEEN   An elephant that sticks to the roof of your mouth.

(PICKLES removes red nose with a shrug.)

KING   That reminds me, what is it that's grey, has two big ears, four legs and a trunk?

PICKLES   An elephant?

KING   No, a mouse going on holiday.

PICKLES   I don't –

(PRINCE and PRINCESS enter L., singing.)

PRINCE &   Hickory Dickory Dock,
PRINCESS   Two mice ran up a clock.
                  The clock struck one –
(Each puts on a red nose. Spoken.)   But the other

	one got away. (They shake hands.)
PICKLES	Everybody wants to get in on the act.
QUEEN	I say, I say, I say, it's in all the evening papers!
PICKLES	What's in all the evening papers?
QUEEN	Fish and chips.
ROUND	Waiter! There's a fly in my soup.
RENDER	Well, keep it quiet, sir, or everybody will want one.
JENNY	Waiter! What's this fly doing in my soup?
DAN	The breast stroke, madam.
PRINCESS	Waiter! This egg is bad.
PRINCE	Well, don't blame me, I only laid the table.
RENDER	Waiter! This egg is bad.
ROUND	Well, take out the yolk and it'll be all white.
KING	Oh, an eggshellent yolk.
	(FAIRIES enter like a Chorus line as PICKLES sings.)
PICKLES	I don't wish to know that, Not even for a wage –
CHORUS	Wait and hear our little rhyme –
PICKLES	Kindly leave the –
CHORUS	(all put on red noses. Chanting) Rose are red, Violets are blue, We can row a boat – Canoe?
OTHERS	Ooh!

PICKLES	Well –
	     I do wish to know that,
	     My mind it does engage.

DREAMAWHILE	(entering R.) But I don't wish to know that.

Sc. 8   THE SLEEPING BEAUTY   101

PICKLES	You don't wish to know that?
DREAMAWHILE	I don't wish to know that.
OTHERS	She don't wish to know that! We'll kindly leave the, kindly leave the, Kindly leave the, kindly leave the –
DREAMAWHILE	Kind – ly – leave – the – STAGE! (Demurely.) Kindly leave the stage.

(ALL exit except DREAMAWHILE. Start LIGHT FADE. MUSIC 72.)

Now all is well, their dreams made good,
They'll sleep as peaceful dreamers should.
(She beckons to R. with her wand.)

(The FAIRIES enter, each with a "dream globe". They "place" them in the urn and float off.)

No, wait a bit, that's only six.
Well, here's a pretty sort of fix.
(She looks into urn.)
The Queen's it is has not been found.
'Tis in some corner, I'll be bound.

(Beam of light from a follow spot focused small COMES UP on floor R.)

Ah, yes, there 'tis. Come little dream.

(It moves over to her.)

Are you undamaged, as you seem?

(It moves up and into her cupped hands. Traverse tabs start to close behind DREAMAWHILE.)

The easiest way's I think to try her.

(DIM OUT FOLLOW SPOT as she closes her hands round it. She then "throws" it up and waves her wand to L.)

Come hither, Queen, conduct your choir.

(Start LIGHT FADE UP for Scene 9.)

THE SLEEPING BEAUTY   Part II

Scene 9   Pause for a Minim or Two

Tabs. QUEEN enters L. with arms outstretched as if sleepwalking. DREAMAWHILE produces a conductor's baton and slips it into the QUEEN's hand, then waves her wand to R. and DAFFY enters sleepwalking. DREAMAWHILE produces a piece of sheet music and puts it into DAFFY's paw and tiptoes off R. QUEEN taps on imaginary music stand (knocks from ORCHESTRA) and begins to conduct. DAFFY opens his mouth; EFFECT 18: <u>a tape of a large choir singing the Hallelujah Chorus at full volume.</u> As the QUEEN's conducting becomes increasingly energetic she steps back a pace or two and crashes into pros arch. DAFFY closes mouth and tape stops.

QUEEN   Ow! There, I've broken my dream.   (Rubs head tenderly.)   My nut too, I think. And it was such a lovely dream, if only I could remember what it was.

DAFFY   (tries to point out his music to her)

QUEEN   Wait a minute, dear.   (Looks at baton.) This should give me a clue. One handed knitting? No. Half a Chinese meal? No. Well, what could it have been?   (Waggling baton.)   I mean, what's the use of — of course! I was conducting a massed choir. Oh, if only I could have a really massed choir of about five hundred and thirty voices, (Or whatever the auditorium contains.)   but where would I find five hundred and —

DAFFY   (nudges her and points to AUDIENCE)

QUEEN   (swiftly counts AUDIENCE)   What a coincidence, exactly five hundred and thirty.

DAFFY   (points to pit)

QUEEN   And an orchestra to boot. Well, I must quickly dream up a song for you all to sing now.   (She closes eyes.)

(Tabs open to reveal a frontcloth the whole of which looks like an enormous piece of sheet music with the words and music (top line only), and entitled

Sc. 9 THE SLEEPING BEAUTY 103

"HALLELUJAH CHORUS". One note is detachable Velcro)

DAFFY (nudges her and points to cloth)

QUEEN Just a moment, dear.

DAFFY (nudges harder and points again)

QUEEN (opening eyes) Yes, dear, I'm trying to dream up – (Sees cloth.) – I have! Well, I'll see how it goes. Thank you, Charlie.

<u>MUSIC 73.</u> "HALLELUJAH CHORUS"

Hallelujah! I'm the one who knows.
Hallelujah! That's the way it goes.
If you can't read music and you make a lot of
 fuss,
I'll stop conducting all you lot and I'll conduct
 a bus.

Oh yes, they'll be able to pick that up in no time, won't they?

DAFFY (nods)

QUEEN We'll start with tutti. That means all of you. I'll count you in. (She counts two beats and lets them sing a few bars.) Oh, no, no, no. I said tutti. There was hardly a tut, let alone a utti. Perhaps you'd better loosen up a bit first, I'll take a note at random. (Takes detachable note from cloth.) Now this is – er – (Looks at it and turns it over.) What is it, Charlie?

CONDUCTOR A-natural.

QUEEN A natural what, dear?

CONDUCTOR I mean, that's the note. Listen. (He indicates for the note to be played.) There, it sounds like that.

QUEEN (putting her note to her ear and shaking it) This one doesn't. It must be a dud. You sound your one again and they can all sing it.

(The note is sounded.)

(Singing it.) Ah! That's it. All of you open your

mouths wider. I should be able to count one thousand and sixty tonsils. (Alter number as appropriate.) That's better. Now we'll try the song again.

(They sing song through once.)

Not bad, but I caught one or two bassos who weren't being very profundo and there was still a nasty touch of the pianissimos all round. Let's try again.

(They sing song through again.)

Very good. Now I've just had a startlingly original idea. No, I have, really. I want to see which sings better, girl sopranos or boy sopranos and I'm going to ask a representative selection up here to find out. Could you see if you could find me any other dreamers to help them up, Daffy?

DAFFY (nods and claps paws)

(HOUSE LIGHTS UP. PICKLES and DAN appear through pass door R. of auditorium and SIR ROUND and SIR RENDER through door at L. and they encourage and help children up. KING wanders onstage R.)

KING Can I help with the competition?

QUEEN Oh yes, Archibald, you can look after the girl sopranos. I was going to ask Lord Dan, but perhaps it's safer not. I'll look after the boys.

(Ad lib competition, which almost always has to be declared a draw. PICKLES, DAN and CHAMPIONS then help children back to their seats.)

Well, while you're all going back let's see what the senior members of the choir can do. (She leads adults in singing until all the children are back.)

(HOUSE OUT. DAN, PICKLES and CHAMPIONS come on stage over cat walk steps.)

Right, last time. We haven't got many years sleep left, so sing it like a very loud lullaby to send us all off.

(Close traverse tabs and fly cloth as song sheet is sung

Sc. 10 THE SLEEPING BEAUTY

    for last time. ALL exit R. on last few bars.
    BLACKOUT. MUSIC 74.)

    Scene 10   Ye Olde Stirrup Cup

    Half set, backed by a gauze cloth representing a huge tangly thicket. Concealed entrance in it L.C. Inn Piece in front of it at R., with sign on it or hanging out reading "YE OLDE STIRRUP CUP". Practical door in Inn piece.

    LIGHTS UP sufficiently to reveal DREAMAWHILE dozing R.C. seated on a large toadstool. Her dandelion clock is R. of her. EFFECT 19 . Clock rings, the dandelion head comes out and waggles. She awakens drowsily. Start dawn rise FADE UP.

DREAMAWHILE   Ah there, the hundred years is up.
    (Points wand at clock and it is pulled off R.)
    And in Ye Olde Stirrup Cup
    Prince Ferdinand, no more a dream,
    Awaits the rising sun's first beam
    To join his party and away,
    A-hunting pleasantly all day.
    A course, though, which I shall prevent
    And lure him on a diff'rent scent.
    For lo, that tangly thicket hedge
    Girts the very castle's edge
    Where Princess Beauty sleeping lies.
    Therefore I shall myself disguise
    And, as a servant of the Inn
    Advanc'd in years with toothless grin,
    Her presence there I shall let fall
    And, with many a nudge withal,
    Urge him to her swift release.   (She rises.)

    (End of FADE UP.)

    So to my task for night doth cease.

Poor Carabosse, she will be mad,
She doesn't know my plans, how sad!
(She skips off above Inn.)

(We hear a cackle of laughter from the toadstool which swivels round and reveals itself to be CARABOSSE.)

CARABOSSE Yes, very sad, my sweet – for you!
Oh dear, what naughty things I do!
Well, I never – disguises, eh?
That is a game that two can play.
First a toadstool, so now I'll be –

(Sounds of activity within Inn.)

Ah, that you'll have to wait and see!
(She runs cackling off L.)

(CHORUS enter from Inn, as two Inn Maidservants, some members of the hunt and four hearty hunting PRINCESSES.)

MUSIC 75.   "THE ROYAL HUNT"

CHORUS Yoicks and tallyho!
A-huntin'-huntin' we will go.
Our Prince is here to lead the show,
And all of us adore him.

PRINCESSES We've come from far and wide
To try to ride at the Prince's side,
We're not just huntin' with the Prince,
We're also huntin' for him!

CHORUS Yoicks and hark away!
There's not a horse to say us 'neigh',
When we go out to hunt today
As well as we are able.

PRINCESSES What a lift for the huntin' life
To be a huntin' Prince's wife.
So matrimonial thoughts are rife
In every huntin' stable.

ALL Yoicks and tallyho!
A-huntin'-huntin' we will go.
Without a hint of silly shyness

Sc. 10   THE SLEEPING BEAUTY

We all salute his Royal Highness.

(The PRINCE enters from Inn. The HUNTERS bow and the MAIDS, with deep lovelorn sighs, curtsey. During following scene they drift off, the MAIDS into Inn and the HUNTERS L. and R.)

PRINCE Good morning. (Giving a little bow to PRINCESSES.) Good morning, Your Highnesses.

PRINCESSES (curtsying) Good morning, Your Highness.
(They cluster eagerly round him each trying to push the others away.)

PRINCE A very fine day.

PRINCESSES Very fine, indeed.

PRINCE Perhaps a little close, though.

(He breaks away, but 1st PRINCESS holds onto his arm and pulls him to one side.)

1st PRINCESS A little walk might clear your head.

2nd PRINCESS (taking over and pulling another way) A little talk might cool you down.

3rd PRINCESS (doing likewise) A little ride without the crowd.

4th PRINCESS (the largest, doing likewise) A little – well, just little me.

PRINCE (is nonplussed for a moment then is struck by an idea) You're perfectly right. I'll meet you in the arbour by the garden gate as soon as I've got rid of the others.

(Smirking, 4th PRINCESS runs off U.R.)

1st PRINCESS (moving in again) Your Highness –

PRINCE Ssh, not a word to the others. I'll join you in the orchard shortly.

(Simpering, 1st PRINCESS runs off D.L.)

2nd PRINCESS (moving in) Your –

PRINCE Just the one I was hoping for. Wait for me alone in the shrubbery.

	(Smirking and simpering 2nd PRINCESS runs off D.R.)
3rd PRINCESS	(running to him with outstretched arms) At last –
PRINCE	(dodging aside) At last, indeed. The stables in five minutes, where we can be away from the others.
3rd PRINCESS	But there aren't any others here.
PRINCE	You never know when there will be. The stables.
3rd PRINCESS	But there's all those ostlers.
PRINCE	Very unobservant, ostlers.
3rd PRINCESS	And horses.
PRINCE	No horse has ever taken the least notice of me. Believe me the stables is the place – er are the places – How about the conservatory?
3rd PRINCESS	Oh, yes! (Exits ecstatic above Inn.)
PRINCE	At least that should keep her busy looking, there isn't one. And I'm not too sure about the arbour, the orchard or the shrubbery either. Really, I've behaved disgracefully, but they've hardly given me a minute's peace all week. Well, ever since my father sent me on this hunting trip. "Nothing like hunting for finding a wife," he said, "so don't you dare return till you've chosen a suitable Princess." Oh, very firm the old man was. The trouble is I know exactly the girl I want to marry, but she doesn't seem to exist, except in my dreams.

<u>MUSIC 76.</u>   "SHE'S ALL I EVER DREAMED"

>   She's all I ever dreamed
>   As soft as summer rain,
>   With hair like Autumn corn,
>   And fingers like the petals of a flower.
>   She is the poetry of every waking hour.
>
>   She is my every thought,
>   With laughter in her eyes
>   And music in her voice,
>   A smile that makes the sun to lose its light,
>   And all the radiance of the starshine in the
>   night.

Sc. 10 THE SLEEPING BEAUTY

> I dream of beauty immortal
> And love beside me forever.
> Her words are laughter, the call of a bird,
> Her laughter the sound of the loveliest song
>   ever heard.
>
> The gentleness of dawn,
> The splendour of the rose,
> The peace that only love eternal knows –
> She's all I ever dreamed.

(Sighs.) But what use are dreams unless they come true? Well, well, I'll have a drink to cheer me up. (Calls.) Anyone there?

(2 MAIDS run on from above Inn and curtsey.)

BOTH   Your Highness?

PRINCE   I'd like –

(Both sigh with deep longing.)

(Moving away.) Er-hm. I'd like –

BOTH   Oh, so would we.

PRINCE   No, no, girls, what I want's –

(Enter DREAMAWHILE from above Inn as a very aged servant, like a comic Victorian maid-servant, carrying a goblet on a tray.)

DREAMAWHILE   (in assumed old voice) Some wine.

1st MAID   Well, who call'd you to serve?

BOTH   He's mine!

DREAMAWHILE   You saucy baggages, be off!
I'm the one to serve this toff.

(They sniff haughtily and move to Inn, turning back to give a last sigh before they exit. DREAMAWHILE moves to PRINCE very slowly indeed. He observes her snail's pace with wonder.)

I'm rather slow, 'tis my rheumatics.
(Aside.) So useful, amateur dramatics.

PRINCE	Don't rush, I'm in no urgent need. You must be very old indeed.
DREAMAWHILE	The oldest here for miles around, But still in wind and limb I'm sound. (She totters.)
	(PRINCE moves hurriedly to steady her.)
	Thank 'ee. Your drink I nearly dropp'd, But only half of it's been slopp'd. (Gives him goblet and pours the spilt half into it from tray.)
	(PRINCE looks at it with distaste.)
	Just now your hopes I overheard, Which in my head a mem'ry stirr'd Of a legend now known to few. It said, and many thought 'twas true, That such a Princess as you crave Lies bewitch'd in a living grave, Sleeping there for many a year, And scarce a stone's throw from right here.
PRINCE	But why then has she not been found?
DREAMAWHILE	Because that hedge – and 'tis renown'd, The thickest thicket in the world! – Around a castle wall is curl'd. And there she waits for one who'll dare Brave the hedge and the perils there And with a kiss wake her at last To end the spell upon her cast.
PRINCE	Your story stirs, yet makes me grieve, Gives me to doubt, yet still believe. One thing is sure, I'd like to try, To prove I'm brave enough to.
	(As he moves towards thicket he is stopped by CARABOSSE who enters L. as a besmocked and bewhiskered old gaffer bent over a gnarled stick, to the consternation of DREAMAWHILE.)
CARABOSSE	Why? 'Tis stuff and nonsense, ev'ry word,

Sc. 10   THE SLEEPING BEAUTY   111

                    A silly feckless tale she's heard.
                    And I should know, for I am, sir,
                    Much older than the likes of her.
                    Ninety today.

DREAMAWHILE   Don't make me laugh.

CARABOSSE   I am!

DREAMAWHILE   I'm ninety and a half.

CARABOSSE   Well, there's no Princess nor a castle,
                    The whole thing is of lies a parcel.

PRINCE   Perhaps you're right, and yet, you know -

4th PRINCESS   (off R.)
                    Your Highness!

1st PRINCESS   (off D.L.)   Prince!

2nd PRINCESS   (off D.R.)   Princey!

3rd PRINCESS   (off above Inn)   Hello!

PRINCE   It would almost a try be worth
                    In case those four run me to earth.

DREAMAWHILE   (producing a locket on chain and putting it round his neck)
                    Then take this locket as a charm.
                    (Aside.)   'Twill see he does not come to harm.
                  (To PRINCE.)   'Twas given me by my old pa,
                  Who had it from his dear old ma.
                  He said she said the portrait there
                  Shew'd the Princess.

                  (CARABOSSE makes a covert magic pass with her stick. Music sting.)

PRINCE   (opening locket)   Which portrait, where?
                  There isn't one.

DREAMAWHILE   (flashing a dagger-filled look at CARABOSSE)
                        Ah, it's this light
                  Tilt it this way.

                  (He does, she makes a magic pass. Double music sting.)
                      There, now that's right.

PRINCE	This face I know not, yet it seems I've seen it in a thousand dreams, And pledg'd to it my heart and mind. Now I'll not rest till her I find. (Starts towards thicket.)
CARABOSSE	Stop! In that hedge much danger lies!
PRINCE	(drawing sword) What's that to me for such a prize! (He exits into thicket.)
	(LIGHTS FADE to spots on the two FAIRIES.)
DREAMAWHILE	(starting to remove disguise) Well tried, but now you'd best give up.
CARABOSSE	(stripping off beard etc.) You do too soon of triumph sup.
DREAMAWHILE	But now the tale is all but done.
CARABOSSE	This spinning tale is not yet spun, I've other spinners near at hand To spin the final fatal strand.
DREAMAWHILE	What, spinning maidens? I've lost track.
CARABOSSE	No, spinning widows – all in black!
	(BLACKOUT. They exit. Strike Inn piece. <u>MUSIC 77.</u> FADE UP LIGHTS behind gauze to reveal Scene 11.)

Scene 11   In the Thick of the Thickest Thicket

Thicket gauze   to open, 2nd thicket gauze behind that and behind that gauze of castle walls with gateway L.C. and web over gateway.

Behind 1st gauze we see PRINCE FERDINAND engaged in a balletic struggle with CHORUS as BRIAR, BLACKTHORN, etc. Fly 1st gauze as he manages to

Sc. 11 THE SLEEPING BEAUTY

overcome them and they exit. Start to FADE UP LIGHTS behind 2nd gauze.

PRINCE
The thicket seems alive, it clutches and tears at me like a wounded beast. (Sees castle walls through 2nd gauze.) At last, the castle walls! I'm almost there. And there's a gateway.

(Fly 2nd gauze as he moves forward and we see gateway is straddled by huge spider's web.)

But what's this?

(CARABOSSE appears L.)

CARABOSSE
Just the gatekeepers home sweet home.
But if through here you'd like to roam,
Why then you'll have to pay their toll,
I'll summon them.

(She plucks a rope-like strand of the web. A deep pluck'd twang sounds and, if possible, one of CHORUS as a large black tarantula appears scuttling down web. Two others come on from R. and one from L.)

Sounds like a knoll.
And so it is! Their toll is high,
It is the life of all who try
To pass through here. I'm bound to say
They'll be delighted if you'll pay,
Poor widow spinners all in black,
Or would you rather now turn back?

PRINCE
I fear such beasts, but e'en such fear
Will never make me turn from here.

CARABOSSE
You give their appetite a zest!
(To TARANTULAS.)
Come, do your worst!

PRINCE
And I - my best!

(MUSIC 78. Spider ballet, in which the PRINCE eventually overcomes the spiders. As he triumphantly slashes at the web with his sword CARABOSSE exits L. with a howl of rage. The web parts or is flown. Exit PRINCE R. MUSIC 79. LIGHTS UP behind castle wall gauze to reveal Scene 12.)

THE SLEEPING BEAUTY   Part II

Scene 12   The Royal Palace

As in Scene 7 except that in some places the castle walls have crumbled and branches of the hedge peep in here and there, particularly briars with roses blooming on them. There are also some cobwebs, one of which attaches the KING to the throne, and generally there is a dusty look to the Palace.

DIM LIGHT to open. All the sleepers in the same poses as at the end of Scene 7. KING and QUEEN give a little snore each, then swallow and settle peacefully again. The CHAMPIONS' heads on JENNY's shoulders stir a little. DAFFY gives a couple of snorts. PICKLES smiles and gives a little giggle. DAN gives a sigh. All is quiet for a moment then the PRINCE enters U.C. and looks about him with wonder.

PRINCE   It is true, a sleeping Palace. The dogs in the court-yard, the doves in the dovecote, the blacksmith and the horse whose shoe he mends all, all asleep. And now in here –   (Shakes gently whoever happens to be nearest him.)   – yes, fast asleep.   (Looks at locket.)   And you, my love, do you sleep still? (He moves to pull a tattered drapery aside from the window L., it collapses and a shaft of light comes onto the PRINCESS.)

(MUSIC 80. "YOU'LL SEE" Reprise.)

Yes, there's my Princess, there's the love of my dreams. Be now the love of my life, reality's more sweet than any dream.   (He slowly approaches the couch and falls on one knee beside it and leans forward to kiss the PRINCESS softly.)

(For a moment nothing happens, then the PRINCESS' eyelids flutter, she sees the PRINCE and sits up.)

PRINCESS   Do I dream still? No, my Dreamdust was all gone. Then you are real, you have come true my – my Ferdinand.

PRINCE   You know my name?

PRINCESS   Oh yes, I've known you for a long long time.

Sc. 12   THE SLEEPING BEAUTY   115

PRINCE &   Day breaks:
PRINCESS   Love has opened our eyes;
    And now with ecstasy and wonder and surprise
    We see, we see, we see!

(While they gaze at each other enter DREAMAWHILE
D.R. in front of gauze. Start to FADE UP LIGHTS to
reveal other sleepers more. MUSIC 81.)

DREAMAWHILE   Their dreams come true, my task is done,
    This twain in rapture are as one.
    So now all's ended as it ought,
    There's but to wake the sleeping court.
    (She waves wand.)

(Fly castle walls gauze cloth. She points wand at
LORD DAN who yawns and stretches slowly; then at
PICKLES, who sits up with a sharp movement
displacing some of the dust that has settled on him
(Fuller's earth) and sneezes; then at the CHAMPIONS
and JENNY, who wakes first and seeks to remove the
weight of their heads from her shoulders; then at
DAFFY, who stretches and shakes himself like a dog;
and lastly at the KING and QUEEN who yawn and
stretch lazily. DREAMAWHILE is about to go, but
stops and smiles.)

There's one last dreamer, sleeping sound.
(Points wand at Feather boa.)
Thou too shalt have thy wish - when found.
(She laughs and runs off R.)

(MUSIC 82. Boa 4 wiggles into life. AUDIENCE
shout.)

QUEEN   (still not quite awake)   What? What's the matter?
What's all the - ? Me feather boa!   (She leaps
up and almost gets it before it disappears into its hole.)
I've caught it! I've -   (Her finger is apparently
stuck in hole.)   I've been caught meself! Oo,
it's tickling me. No, it's stopped now.   (Tugs
finger out.)   Well, where's it gooooooooone!
There's something crawling uuuuuuuuuuuup!
(From her contortions whatever it is apparently moves
up the back of her legs and her back to her neck where

	she grabs with a hand.) It's that naughty Fluffy! (She pulls out a thin fur stole.) You clever thing, you've turned into a Minky! (Moving to throne.) Look, Archibald.
KING	(trying to detach himself from the cobweb) Yes, dear. I do think the staff should dust occasionally.
PICKLES	(brushing himself and raising another cloud of dust) It is rather - ah - ah - ahchoo!
JENNY	Oi! (She manages to jerk her shoulders free.)
	(SIR ROUND and SIR RENDER topple into each other and bump heads.)
BOTH	Ow!
ROUND	Render! You're half asleep on the job, lad. We're supposed to be takin' this gel to the dungeons.
DAN	But wait! Sire, the Princess, look!
KING	(not looking. Sadly) I know, she's -
QUEEN	Archibald, she's not!
PICKLES	She's awake!
ROUND	She lives!
RENDER	She - oh, how nice!
DAFFY	(gives two exultant puffs of smoke)
KING	Then the spell is broken! But who are you, young man?
PRINCE	The one who was fortunate enough to break it, sir, when I woke your daughter with a kiss.
QUEEN	What a lovely idea. Anyone care to make quite sure I'm awake? (Closes eyes.)
DAFFY	(obliges)
QUEEN	Ah, Daffy. Well, I love you too, dear.
KING	May I ask your name, sir?
PRINCE	Prince Ferdinand, your Majesty. And may I ask - most humbly - for your daughter's hand?

Sc. 12 THE SLEEPING BEAUTY

KING	If my daughter will accept you –
PRINCESS	With all my heart.
KING	Then take her, my boy, with our blessings and our deepest thanks.
PICKLES	Princess, I'm very happy for you.
PRINCESS	Thank you, dear Jester.
PICKLES	And I hope – (Remembers something.) I hope there'll be plenty of custard pies at the wedding feast.
KING	The wedding feast! Chamberlain, see that all preparations are made forthwith, and plenty of buns fifthwith.
DAN	At once, sire. There is one little difficulty, though. Her Highness should have a Maid of Honour in attendance but – er –
KING	What? Oh, well she can be released now, of course.
	(CHAMPIONS release JENNY.)
JENNY	Cor, thanks. And can I really be a Maid of Honour?
DAN	Yes, unless – (He whispers in her ear.)
	(JENNY looks at DAN a moment then nods happily.)
	Slight amendment, sire. (Producing and putting a ring on JENNY's finger.) There'll be a Matron of Honour in attendance.
KING	Splendid, then on with the royal wedding! Pity we woke up one day too late for my birthday but – My birthday! He-he! I missed it! Ha-ha! I missed my birthday! (Goes into peals of uproarious laughter.)
	(CHORUS run on L. and R.)
QUEEN	Archibald!
PRINCESS	Father!
DAN & CHAMPIONS	Sire!
CHORUS	Your Majesty!

QUEEN	Archibald, you're laughing!
KING	I know, because I missed my birthday by one day! (Again is overcome.)
QUEEN	But what's so funny about that?
KING	Don't you see? It was my one hundred and fiftieth birthday, so now I'm a hundred and fifty and a day. Carabosse's curse on me is broken too! (Goes into more peals of laughter.)
	(ALL join with him laughing.)
	I'm old and I really am merry at last. (Calling.) Bring me a bowl of wine and a pipe and let's have some music!
	(1st, 2nd, 3rd and 4th CHORUS join their groups, 5th and 6th CHORUS move a throne D.C., which KING sits on, and then they exit as do the remainder of the CHORUS. Close traverse tabs, fly in frontcloth for following scene.)

<u>MUSIC 83.</u>   "OLD KING COLE"

ALL	Old King Cole was a merry old soul, And a merry old soul was he.
KING	Old King Cole -
ALL	Old King Cole -
KING	Was a merry old soul -
ALL	Was a merry old soul - And a merry old soul was he.
	(5th CHORUS enters R. with a churchwarden pipe which she gives to KING during following and exits.)
KING	He called for his pipe - He called for his pipe -
	(6th CHORUS enters L. with a small bowl which she gives to KING during following and exits.)
KING	And he called for his bowl -
ALL	And he called for his bowl -

Sc. 12 THE SLEEPING BEAUTY

(7th and 8th CHORUS enter L. with 3 prop violins and bows which they give to QUEEN, PICKLES and 1st CHORUS and exit.)

    And he called for his fiddlers three.
    Every fiddler he had a fine fiddle,
    And a very fine fiddle had he.

QUEEN, PICKLES & 1st CHORUS   Twee, tweedle-dee, tweedle-dee went the fiddlers.

(They mime playing violins to music.)

ALL   Oh, there's none so rare as can compare
With King Cole and his fiddlers three!

KING   Old King Cole -

ALL   Old King Cole - etc.

(5th CHORUS enters R. with a pipe for KING and exits as before; 6th CHORUS enters L. with a bowl, but a larger one, which she gives to KING and exits as before, and at the appropriate point 9th and 10th CHORUS enter R. with 3 prop harps which they give to PRINCE, PRINCESS and 2nd CHORUS and exit.)

    And he called for his harpers three.
    Every harper he had a fine harp,
    And a very fine harp had he.

PRINCE, PRINCESS & 2nd CHORUS   Twang, twang-a-twang, twang-a-twang went the harpers.

(They mime playing harps to music.)

QUEEN, PICKLES & 1st CHORUS   Twee, tweedle-dee, tweedle-dee went the fiddlers.

(They mime to music.)

ALL   Oh, there's none so rare as can compare
With King Cole and his harpers three!

KING   Old King Cole -

ALL   Old King Cole - etc.

(5th CHORUS enters with another pipe, 6th with a still larger bowl so that KING has increasing difficulty in balancing them all, and 7th and 8th enter L. with 3 pipes (musical) which they give to ROUND, RENDER

	and 3rd CHORUS and exit.)
	And he called for his pipers three. Every piper he had a fine pipe, And a very fine pipe had he.
ROUND, RENDER & 3rd CHORUS	Then tootle, tootle-too, tootle-too went the pipers.
	(They mime playing pipes to music.)
PRINCE, PRINCESS & 2nd CHORUS	Twang, twang-a-twang, twang-a-twang went the harpers.
	(They mime to music.)
QUEEN, PICKLES & 1st CHORUS	Twee, tweedle-dee, tweedle-dee went the fiddlers.
	(They mime to music.)
ALL	Oh, there's none so rare as can compare With King Cole and his pipers three!
KING	Old King Cole -
ALL	Old King Cole - etc.
	(5th CHORUS enters with a 4th pipe, 6th with a very large bowl, 9th and 10th with 3 toy drums and drumsticks which they give to DAN, JENNY and 4th CHORUS, but remain on.)
	And he called for his drummers three. Every drummer he had a fine drum, And a very fine drum had he.
DAN, JENNY & 4th CHORUS	Then rub-a-dub, a dub, rub-a-dub went the drummers.
	(They mime drumming to music.)
	(Rest of CHORUS enter.)
ROUND, RENDER & 3rd CHORUS	Then tootle, tootle-too, tootle-too went the pipers.
	(They mime to music.)
PRINCE, PRINCESS & 2nd CHORUS	Twang, twang-a-twang, twang-a-twang went the harpers.
	(They mime to music.)

Sc. 12   THE SLEEPING BEAUTY   121

QUEEN, PICKLES & 1st CHORUS	Twee, tweedle-dee, tweedle-dee went the fiddlers. (They mime to music.)
ALL	Oh, there's none so rare as can compare With King Cole and his drummers, And his pipers, And his harpers, And his fiddlers –
KING & 5th - 10th CHORUS	Three! (Sustained during following 4 lines.)
QUEEN, PICKLES & 1st CHORUS	Tweedle-dee!
PRINCE, PRINCESS & 2nd CHORUS	Twang-a-twang!
ROUND, RENDER & 3rd CHORUS	Tootle-too!
DAN, JENNY & 4th CHORUS	Rub-a-dub!
ALL	There's none so rare as can compare With King Cole and all of we.

(BLACKOUT. ALL exit, 2 of CHORUS striking throne. Open traverse tabs.)

Scene 13   Family Reunion

Front cloth. Scene 2 cloth could be used again.

LIGHTS UP. Enter DREAMAWHILE R.

DREAMAWHILE   A good day's work, well – a hundred years,
              Oh, and eighteen more as well, my dears.
              Well, you would never think, I trow,
              That we first met so long ago.   (Yawns.)
              I feel some sleep then is my due,
              For ev'ry dream has now come true.

CARABOSSE	(off L.) There's one that's not.
DREAMAWHILE	Who's that did call?
	(Puppet doll of CARABOSSE appears round pros arch L. It wears a veil.)
CARABOSSE	(voice) Me over here upon the wall. Since all my hopes you have quite sunk I feel so mortified I've shrunk. And what is worse, cannot recall How to enlarge myself at all. Would you help?
DREAMAWHILE	I'm not sure I ought, With all the mischief you have wrought.
CARABOSSE	Oh, please.
DREAMAWHILE	No.
CARABOSSE	Please, dear –
DREAMAWHILE	Yes?
CARABOSSE	Dear – sister.
DREAMAWHILE	When she says that I can't resist her. So long have we been split in twain I thought you'd ne'er say that again. But gladly for a sister's sake The necessary steps I'll take. (Waves wand.)
	(BLACKOUT. FLASH. LIGHTS UP. CARABOSSE is revealed full size, also veiled.)
	Now, sister dear – but why the veil?
CARABOSSE	'Tis all part of my sorry tale, It hides my dream that's unfulfill'd, My heartfelt hope which can't be still'd.
DREAMAWHILE	And what is that?
CARABOSSE	Beauty – that's all. Envy of thine 'twas caus'd my fall.

	And yet, despite my magic power,
	I still look like a tragic shower.
	I just now tried one last endeavour –
	It's made me look much worse than ever!
	I wonder, would you have a go?
DREAMAWHILE	But for immortals, as you know,
	Beauty lies deeper than the skin,
	For us it must grow from within,
	That's something only you can do.
CARABOSSE	Alas then, my dream won't come true.
DREAMAWHILE	Yes. Give yourself, to know that bliss,
	A moral beauty treatment, Sis.

(Close traverse tabs. Fly out cloth.)

MUSIC 84.   "SKIN DEEP"

Beauty lies deep in every person,
Be she a better, be she a worse 'un.
Under the surface loveliness there must be.

CARABOSSE   I'm very pleased with this information.
I'd like to have your cooperation
Just to find out if beauty lies deep in me.

DREAMAWHILE   If the challenge you would take up,
Change your mode of moral make-up;
Then one day you'll find you'll wake up
Well endowed.

CARABOSSE   If I say things like "thank you" and "pardon"
I won't require Elizabeth Arden –

DREAMAWHILE)   I've a   )   (I'm
CARABOSSE   )   You've a) sister then of whom (You're proud.

DREAMAWHILE   You don't require a perfect complexion,
You needn't buy the Paris collection,
Just change direction now to a goal that's high.

CARABOSSE   If you suggest that auto-hypnosis
Might make me have a smaller proboscis
'I'll have a go, sis, I am prepared to try.

DREAMAWHILE   Philanthropic exercises

THE SLEEPING BEAUTY Part II

> In the most discreet disguises
> Often bring surprising prizes
> From the crowd.

(CARABOSSE removes veil and reveals herself as young and beautified.)

CARABOSSE Now I have changed my looks within reason
I've cause to bless the pantomime season

DREAMAWHILE $\left\{\begin{array}{l}\text{You've}\\\text{I've}\end{array}\right\}$ a sister now of whom $\left\{\begin{array}{l}\text{you're}\\\text{I'm}\end{array}\right.$ proud.

CARABOSSE Sing it loud!

DREAMAWHILE Now I have a sister –

CARABOSSE A darling baby sister –

DREAMAWHILE (spoken) You must be joking!

CARABOSSE)
DREAMAWHILE) $\left\{\begin{array}{l}\text{You've}\\\text{I've}\end{array}\right\}$ a sister now of whom $\left\{\begin{array}{l}\text{you're}\\\text{I'm}\end{array}\right.$ proud.

(As they exit, <u>MUSIC 85</u> and open traverse tabs.)

Scene 14   The Royal Wedding Reception

Grand Palace scene with steps down in C. in front of rostrum.

Walk down starts. CHORUS enter in pairs, one from each side on rostrum, take their bow D.C. and back to form diagonal lines L. and R. Principals follow similar procedure, forming diagonal lines in front of them. CARABOSSE from L. backing to L: DREAMAWHILE from R. to R.: ROUND from L. and RENDER from R. to L. and R. respectively: JENNY from R. and DAN from L., both to L.: KING from R. to R.: DAFFY from L. to R.: PICKLES from R. to L.: QUEEN from L. to R. When she has taken her bow <u>MUSIC 86.</u> ALL turn U.C. as PRINCE enters from R. to C. of rostrum and extends an arm for PRINCESS who enters from L. to join him.)

ALL	Hurray!
	(PRINCE and PRINCESS move D.C. to take their bow, then Principals come into line with them and CHORUS move up to line the rostrum.)
PRINCESS	My story ends, my dream's come true.
PRINCE	And so has mine for I've won you.
PICKLES	I lost my love, but won a jest.
DREAMAWHILE	I won the day, (Yawns.) but lost some rest.
CARABOSSE	I lost a foe, but won a sister.
JENNY	I won a man.
DAN	But not a mister. If you're confused then rest assur'd, I merely meant that I'm a lord.
QUEEN	Well, I've won back my feather boa, So really I can't ask for moa!
	(ALL groan except KING who laughs.)
KING	To find that funny proves I've won back laughter.
PRINCESS	So now we'll all live –
ALL	Happy ever after!

MUSIC 87.   GRAND FINALE

That was a wonderful party.
  We thank you for coming;
  Go away laughing and humming,
For that's our delight.
Since all our story is ended
Our leave we must take now.
Since everybody's awake now
We bid you, we bid you, we bid you,
We bid you, we bid you, we bid you –
Good night!

CURTAIN

FURNITURE AND PROPERTY PLOT

PART I

Scene 1

Set on Stage

U.C.   Outside double door, 18 bottles of milk.
R.C.   3 Spinning wheels and stools and spindles of gold thread.
L.C.   2 Thrones.

Feather Boas: these have thin nylon lines attached at each end and threaded through holes in the scenery and through screw-eyes where necessary, except for Boas Nos. 1 and 5.
  Boa 2 - To travel up and down pros arch L.
  Boa 3 - To travel to and fro along top of floats.
  Boa 4 - To travel up and down pros arch R. (This Boa is used for all appearances in subsequent scenes.)
  Boa 5 - To descend from flies. (This will require a small weight on one end.)
  Boa 6 - To move laterally across wing L.
  Boa 7 - To go through window L. of central doors.
  Boa 8 - To appear through keyhole of R. central door and go off R.

Off R.

Shopping basket with old-fashioned motor car bulb horn on handle and a Royal crest on one side of basket. It contains:-	
Large prop leek.	
Outsize prop packet of "Polos".	QUEEN
Pair of roller skates.	QUEEN
6 wands.	CHORUS
A parchment and a quill.	1 of CHORUS

Off L.

Dusters and brooms.	CHORUS
2 cream buns.	KING
King's slipper for right foot, with edible pom-pom (marshmallow).	1st CHORUS GIRL
Silver salver.	1st CHORUS GIRL

FURNITURE AND PROPERTY PLOT

Mediaeval pram with castellations round its
  top containing:-
    Small piece of silvery knitting on large
      wooden needles.
    Blue enamel saucepan.
    A lance bent at right angles.
    Two-handed sword with very short
      blade in a floppy scabbard.
    Old fashioned pistol (practical), with one
      round shot and small bag of powder.   SIR RENDER
Crumpled conical hat.   QUEEN
Feather Boa 1, with nylon line attached to the
  end to pull it offstage, and large fan.   QUEEN
King's slipper for left foot, set on salver during
  scene.   1st CHORUS GIRL
A scroll.   LORD DAN
Large trick sword (with bolt on blade so that
  the blade apparently breaks when bolt is
  released).   SIR ROUND
Trick spiked bludgeon (a trick wand turning
  into a bunch of flowers can be adapted for
  this).   SIR RENDER
Ornate cradle.   CHORUS
Baby doll swathed in long gold robe.   QUEEN
Baby's bottle.   1st CHORUS GIRL

In Flies

  Prop dead chicken.

Personal

SIR ROUND	Sword.
SIR RENDER	Sword, woollen mitten.
DREAMAWHILE	Silver wand.
CARABOSSE	Black wand.

Scene 2

Set on Stage

In Cavern L: Small cauldron over a prop fire.
              A stool and table with playing cards
                 on it.
              Shelves with various phials and

FURNITURE AND PROPERTY PLOT

In Dell R:—
bottles, including one labelled "ZITHER STRINGS" and one "NEWTS TOES": 1 large book labelled "SPELLS": several glasses: pepper pot: bottle of gin: wooden spoon.
Cuckoo-like clock with Vulture to emerge. (Vulture on the end of a thin bamboo cane operated offstage.)
Shelves with similar phials and bottles including those labelled "ZITHER STRINGS" and "NEWTS TOES", and the Dreamdust phial containing gold glitter powder.
Large Dandelion clock, numbered from 1-20 round dial, the hands set between 17 and 18. A dandelion head pops out through its door and waggles. (Also worked by a cane offstage.) The clock is fitted with an electric bell operated offstage.

Off R.

Couch fitted with Shepherd Castors for ease of pushing on and pulling off.
Idiot board on which is written – "HA! HA!"
Idiot board on which is written – "SILENCE"

Off L.

Large triangular suitcase inscribed – "SPINNING JENNY. TRAVELLING SALES CONSULTANT FOR PORTABLE SPINNING WHEELS. H.P. TERMS ARRANGED." It contains a spinning wheel, which for lightness should be made of balsa wood. There is a torch bulb on the tip of the spindle, powered by a concealed battery and operated by a switch on the spinning wheel base.   JENNY
H.P. Form.   JENNY

FURNITURE AND PROPERTY PLOT

Scene 3

Set on Stage

L.C. Dais with tapestry curtains on a frame at the back of it and a 2 ft. post at each corner. On each post is a metal cup to take the canopy poles. The cups are pin-hinged to the posts with nylon line attached to the pins. The other ends of the lines are anchored to the arms of two thrones on the dais so that when the KING and QUEEN pull the lines the canopy will collapse.

Off R.

Posy of flowers.	PRINCESS
Mediaeval bicycle with bell on handlebars and saddle made to look like wood.	QUEEN
Jester's pig's bladder (balloon attached with a coloured string to a stick).	PICKLES
Dreamdust phial with long label attached.	PICKLES
Spinning wheel case with inscriptions removed.	JENNY
Pile of trick plates threaded together with one breakable plate loose on top.	QUEEN
Trolley covered to the ground with a cloth. On trolley:- a plate of practical buns, large milk jug, several teacups and one tiny one with a hole in it going through to a tank underneath. It also has a rubber tube pointing upwards fitted inside it; the other end of the tube is attached to the nozzle of a soda syphon fitted on the upstage side of the trolley.	KING
Trick sword (when withdrawn from scabbard it turns out to be an umbrella which is made so that SIR ROUND can turn it inside out).	SIR ROUND
Dummy suit of armour a replica of SIR RENDER's.	Put on in Blackout

Off L.

Canopy (a lightweight material on four poles of ¾ inch dowelling).	CHORUS
Kitchen boiler (canvas on a lightweight frame painted to look like steel with broken off pipes sticking out of its sides. It must be large enough	

to go over DAFFY and requires handles inside
for him to lift it and a detachable lid he can
perch on his head like a hat).   KING
Lance (not bent).   SIR RENDER

Set as convenient

Mops and brooms for opening number of scene.   CHORUS

Check

SIR ROUND has sword (personal prop).

Scene 4

Set on Stage

On truck — low 3 legged stool.

Off R.

Spinning wheel case as in previous scene
containing spinning wheel.   JENNY

Off L.

Glove puppet doll to represent CARABOSSE
with long black cloak.   CARABOSSE

Check

PRINCESS has Dreamdust phial.

Scene 5

Off R.

Large oil can.   SIR RENDER

Off L.

Clothes horse draped with garments, one
simulating QUEEN's dress, but with sleeves
large enough for KING to get over his legs.
One garment sopping.   KING

Set off as convenient

For opening number of scene:-
  Towels.   CHORUS
  Medicine bottles and large spoon.   LORD DAN

FURNITURE AND PROPERTY PLOT 131

Scene 7

Set on Stage

L.C. Thrones, as in Scene 1.

Off R.

  Couch.   CHORUS

PART II

Scene 8

Set on Stage

D.R. Lectern stand.

Off R.

  Huge book labelled "DREAM REGISTER"   3rd & 4th FAIRIES
  Large quill pen and large ink horn.   5th FAIRY
  Large pair of spectacles and bag labelled
    "DREAM ADJUSTMENTS" containing:-
    2 cartons labelled "CURRANTS", 2 mini
    feather dusters, 2 magnifying glasses, a
    pair of scissors and a needle and thread.   6th FAIRY
  Large white balloon inscribed "DREAM".   To be thrown on
  Towel.   2nd FAIRY
  Book entitled "JOKES".   To be put into
                                                  DREAMAWHILE's hand
  Chains.   DAFFY & QUEEN
  Large head bandage.   SIR RENDER
  Trolley loaded with goodies including
    practical and cotton wool buns and custard
    pies (cardboard plates with whipped up
    shaving cream). Trolley used in KING's
    dream can be used.   5th & 6th FAIRIES
  5 mops.   5 FAIRIES
  Gauze R. props:- Trolley loaded with goodies   KING's dream
                    Chains   DAFFY's dream

Off L.

  Towel.   1st FAIRY

Large head bandage.		SIR ROUND
Gauze L. props:-	Poster advertising "MASSED CHOIR CONCERT TO BE CONDUCTED BY HER MAJESTY THE QUEEN IN PERSON".	QUEEN's dream
	Cartoon balloon coming out of PICKLES' head. Large arrow-pierced heart inscribed in bold letters "PRINCESS".	PICKLES' dream

Check

SIR ROUND and SIR RENDER have swords.

Personal

All taking part in production number – red noses.

Scene 9

Set on Frontcloth

Detachable note (an A-natural) held in place by Velcro.

Personal

DREAMAWHILE	A conductor's baton and a piece of sheet music.

Scene 10

Set on Stage

R.C.   Dreamawhile's dandelion clock.

Off R.

Goblet of wine on a tray.	DREAMAWHILE

Off L.

Gnarled stick.	CARABOSSE

Personal

DREAMAWHILE	A locket on a chain.
PRINCE	Sword.

FURNITURE AND PROPERTY PLOT

Scene 12

Set on Stage

L.C.   Thrones, as in Scene 7. Cobweb fastened to one throne and attached to KING with Velcro.
U.L.C. Tattered drapery over window.
Other cobwebs scattered round.
Fuller's earth dusted over PICKLES.

Off R.

4 churchwarden pipes.	5th CHORUS
3 prop harps.	9th & 10th CHORUS
3 toy drums and drumsticks.	9th & 10th CHORUS

Off L.

4 wine bowls, of succeedingly larger sizes.	6th CHORUS
3 prop violins and bows.	7th & 8th CHORUS
3 musical pipes.	7th & 8th CHORUS

Personal

QUEEN	Thin fur stole concealed down the back of her dress.
DAN	Wedding ring.

Scene 13

Off L.

Puppet doll, veiled.	CARABOSSE

EFFECTS PLOT

PART I

Scene 1

1.	Loud glass crash (bucket of broken glass thrown into second bucket).	Off L.
2.	Sound of rushing wind growing in volume.	Wind Machine off as convenient

Scene 2

3.	Clock chime followed by vulture's croak.	Tape
4.	Alarm clock bell (fitted into dandelion and operated offstage as convenient).	

Scene 3

5.	Bell tinkle (from small handbell).	Off L.
6.	Deep toned bell.	Off R.
7.	Loud glass crash.	Off L.
8.	Loud clattering and banging.	Off L.
9.	Louder clattering and banging.	Off L.
10.	Maroon explosion.	Off R.
11.	Clap of thunder.	Thunder sheet off as convenient
12.	Wind.	Wind machine
13.	Thunder.	Thunder sheet
14.	Sudden squall of wind.	Wind machine

Scene 5

15.	Clanking of armour	Off R.
16.	Sound of cloth ripping, Velcro.	Off R.
17.	Cloth ripping.	Off R.

PART II

Scene 8

18.	"Hallelujah Chorus" sung by large choir at full volume.	Tape

Scene 10

19.	Dandelion clock alarm bell.	Off as convenient

MUSIC PLOT

PART I

1. Overture.

Scene 1

2.	"THIS TIME OF DAY", Opening Chorus	DAN & CHORUS
3.	KING's entrance music	Orchestra
4.	"WHENEVER I LAUGH"	KING
5.	CHAMPIONS' entrance music	Orchestra
6.	"ONCE UPON A TIME"	SIR ROUND & SIR RENDER
7.	QUEEN's entrance music	Orchestra
8.	"CHORES"	QUEEN
9.	DAFFY's entrance music	Orchestra
10.	Feather Boa tune	Orchestra
11.	Feather Boa tune, reprise 10	Orchestra
12.	Feather Boa tune, reprise 10	Orchestra
13.	Feather Boa tune, reprise 10	Orchestra
14.	Feather Boa tune, reprise 10	Orchestra
15.	Feather Boa tune, reprise 10	Orchestra
16.	Feather Boa tune, reprise 10	Orchestra
17.	"CHORES", reprise 8	QUEEN
18.	Procession music, reprise 5	Orchestra
19.	Procession music, reprise 5	Orchestra
20.	Fanfare	Orchestra
21.	Fairy music	Orchestra
22.	Spell music	Orchestra
23.	Scene 1 Finale (continue, orchestra only as link to next scene)	Ensemble

Scene 2

24.	Scene 2 opening music	Orchestra
25.	Fairy music, reprise 21	Orchestra
26.	Sales talk accompaniment	JENNY
27.	"SPELLBOUND" (continue, orchestra only, as link to next scene)	DREAMAWHILE, JENNY, CARABOSSE, PICKLES

Scene 3

28.	"HAPPY BIRTHDAY"	Ensemble
29.	"HAPPY BIRTHDAY", reprise 28	PRINCESS & Ensemble

30.	Feather Boa tune, reprise 10	Orchestra
31.	Dreamdust music	Orchestra
32.	Dreamdust music, reprise 31	Orchestra
33.	Dreamdust music, reprise 31	Orchestra
34.	Dreamdust music, reprise 31	Orchestra
35.	Dreamdust music, reprise 31	Orchestra
36.	Dreamdust music, reprise 31	Orchestra
37.	"YOU'LL SEE"	PRINCE & PRINCESS
38.	Mysterioso music	Orchestra
39.	Mysterioso music, reprise 38	Orchestra
40.	Mysterioso music, reprise 38	Orchestra
41.	"REASONS FOR LOVE"	DAN & JENNY
42.	Feather Boa tune, reprise 10	Orchestra
43.	Fanfare, reprise 20	Orchestra
44.	Suitors' entrance march, reprise 5	Orchestra
45.	"RAIN, RAIN" (continue, orchestra only, as link to next scene)	PICKLES & CHORUS

Scene 4

46.	Whooshy music	Orchestra
47.	Spell music, reprise 22	Orchestra
48.	Spell music, reprise 22	Orchestra
49.	Link to next scene, reprise 22	Orchestra

Scene 5

50.	"COUGH AD SDEEZE"	DAN & CHORUS
51.	Feather Boa tune, reprise 10	Orchestra
52.	Link to next scene, reprise 22	Orchestra

Scene 6

53.	Spinning music, reprise 22	Orchestra
54.	Link to next scene, reprise 22	Orchestra

Scene 7

55.	"HAPPY BIRTHDAY", reprise 28 sadly	Orchestra
56.	"YOU'LL SEE", reprise 37	PRINCE
57.	Fairy music, reprise 21	Orchestra
58.	Feather Boa tune, reprise 10 becoming sleepy	Orchestra
59.	Creepy music	Orchestra

MUSIC PLOT

60.	Hedge Building Ballet	CARABOSSE & CHORUS
61.	Entr'acte	

PART II

Scene 8

62.	Fairy Ballet	DREAMAWHILE & CHORUS
63.	Fairy music, reprise 21	Orchestra
64.	"THE STUFF OF DREAMS"	PRINCESS
65.	CARABOSSE music, reprise 22	Orchestra
66.	Fairy music, reprise 21	Orchestra
67.	Balloon Dance	KING, QUEEN & PICKLES
68.	Fairy music, reprise 21	Orchestra
69.	"CONFUSION"	PRINCE, PRINCESS DAN & JENNY
70.	Fairy music, reprise 21	Orchestra
71.	"I DON'T WISH TO KNOW THAT", patter production number	Ensemble
72.	Fairy music, reprise 21 (continue as link to next scene)	Orchestra

Scene 9

73.	"HALLELUJAH CHORUS", song sheet	QUEEN & AUDIENCE
74.	Link to next scene, reprise 21	Orchestra

Scene 10

75.	"THE ROYAL HUNT"	CHORUS
76.	"SHE'S ALL I EVER DREAMED"	PRINCE
77.	Link to next scene	Orchestra

Scene 11

77.	Continued as first fight and under dialogue with segue into 78	Orchestra

MUSIC PLOT

78.	Spider Ballet	PRINCE, CARABOSSE & CHORUS
79.	Link to next scene	Orchestra

Scene 12

79.	Continued as opening music	Orchestra
80.	"YOU'LL SEE", reprise 37	PRINCE & PRINCESS
81.	Fairy music, reprise 21	Orchestra
82.	Feather Boa tune, reprise 10	Orchestra
83.	"OLD KING COLE" (continue, orchestra only, as link to next scene)	Ensemble

Scene 13

84.	"SKIN DEEP"	DREAMAWHILE & CARABOSSE
85.	Link to next scene, reprise 2	Orchestra

Scene 14

85.	Continued for walk down	Orchestra
86	Fanfare, reprise 20	Orchestra
87.	Grand Finale	Tutti

www.ingramcontent.com/pod-product-compliance
Ingram Content Group UK Ltd.
Pitfield, Milton Keynes, MK11 3LW, UK
UKHW021843210426
5322IPUK00022B/432